50 Oregon State Recipes for Home

By: Kelly Johnson

Table of Contents

- Oregon Blackberry Jam
- Pacific Northwest Clam Chowder
- Wild Mushroom Risotto
- Salmon with Lemon-Dill Sauce
- Marionberry Pie
- Oregon Hazelnut Crusted Chicken
- Dungeness Crab Cakes
- Pear and Hazelnut Salad
- Oregon Wine-Braised Short Ribs
- Raspberry-Glazed Pork Chops
- Smoked Trout Spread
- Huckleberry Pancakes
- Oregon-style Beef Stroganoff
- Black Cod with Miso
- Grilled Salmon with Teriyaki Sauce
- Oregon Pinot Noir Beef Stew
- Chanterelle Mushroom Soup
- Blackberry Sage Sorbet
- Grilled Asparagus with Lemon
- Hazelnut-Crusted Salmon
- Portlandia-Style Veggie Burger
- Apple Cider Brined Pork Loin
- Oregon Raspberry Balsamic Vinaigrette
- Roasted Beet and Goat Cheese Salad
- Wild Salmon Teriyaki
- Pumpkin Ale Bread
- Oregon Blueberry Cheesecake
- Spiced Apple Cider
- Pan-Seared Sea Bass with Herb Butter
- Marionberry Smoothie
- Creamy Mushroom Pasta
- Grilled Oysters with Garlic Butter
- Oregon Cherry BBQ Sauce
- Roasted Vegetable Medley
- Hazelnut-Coffee Brownies
- Smoked Salmon Bagels

- Pear and Gorgonzola Salad
- Oregon Chardonnay Chicken
- Blackberry-Walnut Bread
- Crab and Corn Chowder
- Huckleberry Crumble Bars
- BBQ Chicken with Oregon Fruit Glaze
- Grilled Portobello Mushrooms
- Marionberry and Almond Tart
- Wild Mushroom and Goat Cheese Pizza
- Oregon Cherry-Lime Sorbet
- Pan-Roasted Duck Breast
- Oregon White Wine Mussels
- Hazelnut-Crusted Trout
- Raspberry Lemon Bars

Oregon Blackberry Jam

Ingredients:

- 4 cups fresh blackberries
- 1 cup granulated sugar
- 1/4 cup lemon juice (about 1 lemon)
- 1 package (1.75 oz) fruit pectin (like Sure-Jell)
- 1/4 cup water

Instructions:

1. **Prepare the Jars:**
   - Sterilize 4 to 5 half-pint canning jars and their lids by boiling them in water for 10 minutes. Keep them hot until ready to use.
2. **Prepare the Fruit:**
   - Wash the blackberries thoroughly and drain. In a large saucepan, mash the blackberries with a potato masher or fork until well crushed.
3. **Cook the Jam:**
   - Stir the lemon juice into the mashed blackberries.
   - In a separate bowl, mix the fruit pectin with 1/4 cup water and stir until dissolved. Add this mixture to the blackberries.
   - Bring the mixture to a boil over medium-high heat, stirring constantly.
   - Once boiling, add the granulated sugar all at once. Stir continuously until the mixture returns to a full, rolling boil.
   - Boil for 1 minute, continuing to stir.
4. **Test the Jam:**
   - To check if the jam has set, place a small spoonful of jam on a cold plate and let it sit for 1 minute. Run your finger through the jam; if it wrinkles and holds its shape, it's ready. If not, continue boiling for an additional 1-2 minutes and test again.
5. **Fill the Jars:**
   - Ladle the hot jam into the prepared jars, leaving about 1/4-inch headspace at the top.
   - Wipe the rims of the jars with a clean, damp cloth to remove any residue.
   - Place the sterilized lids on the jars and screw on the metal bands until they are fingertip-tight.
6. **Process the Jars:**
   - Process the jars in a boiling water bath for 5-10 minutes to ensure they are sealed properly. The water should cover the jars by at least 1 inch.
   - Remove the jars from the water bath and let them cool on a clean towel or rack for 24 hours.
7. **Store:**

- Once cooled, check the seals by pressing the center of each lid. If it doesn't pop back, the jar is sealed. Store sealed jars in a cool, dark place. Unsealed jars can be refrigerated and used within a few weeks.

Enjoy your homemade Oregon Blackberry Jam on toast, in desserts, or as a delightful gift!

Pacific Northwest Clam Chowder

Ingredients:

- 4 slices bacon, diced
- 1 medium onion, finely chopped
- 2 celery stalks, chopped
- 2 cloves garlic, minced
- 1 medium carrot, diced
- 3 tablespoons all-purpose flour
- 2 cups clam juice (or use the juice from the canned clams)
- 2 cups whole milk
- 1 cup heavy cream
- 1 bay leaf
- 1 teaspoon dried thyme
- 2 cups potatoes, peeled and diced
- 2 (6.5 oz) cans chopped clams, with juice
- Salt and black pepper to taste
- 2 tablespoons fresh parsley, chopped (for garnish)
- Lemon wedges (for serving)

Instructions:

1. **Cook the Bacon:**
   - In a large pot or Dutch oven, cook the diced bacon over medium heat until crisp. Remove the bacon pieces with a slotted spoon and set them aside on a paper towel-lined plate. Leave the bacon drippings in the pot.
2. **Sauté Vegetables:**
   - Add the chopped onion, celery, garlic, and carrot to the pot with the bacon drippings. Cook over medium heat until the vegetables are softened, about 5-7 minutes.
3. **Make the Roux:**
   - Sprinkle the flour over the vegetables and stir well to coat. Cook for 1-2 minutes, stirring constantly, until the flour is lightly browned.
4. **Add Liquids:**
   - Gradually stir in the clam juice, ensuring there are no lumps. Bring the mixture to a simmer and cook for 5 minutes.
5. **Add Dairy and Seasonings:**
   - Stir in the milk, heavy cream, bay leaf, and dried thyme. Bring the mixture back to a simmer.
6. **Cook the Potatoes:**
   - Add the diced potatoes to the pot. Simmer for about 10-15 minutes, or until the potatoes are tender.
7. **Add Clams:**

- Stir in the chopped clams with their juice. Simmer for an additional 5 minutes to heat through.
8. **Season and Finish:**
    - Remove the bay leaf. Season the chowder with salt and black pepper to taste.
9. **Serve:**
    - Ladle the chowder into bowls. Garnish with the reserved bacon pieces and fresh parsley. Serve with lemon wedges on the side, if desired.

Enjoy your hearty and comforting Pacific Northwest Clam Chowder!

Wild Mushroom Risotto

Ingredients:

- 6 cups low-sodium chicken or vegetable broth
- 2 tablespoons olive oil
- 1 tablespoon unsalted butter
- 1 medium onion, finely chopped
- 2 cloves garlic, minced
- 2 cups wild mushrooms (e.g., shiitake, cremini, porcini), sliced
- 1 1/2 cups Arborio rice
- 1/2 cup dry white wine
- 1/2 cup freshly grated Parmesan cheese
- 1/4 cup heavy cream (optional for extra creaminess)
- 2 tablespoons fresh parsley, chopped
- Salt and black pepper to taste

Instructions:

1. **Prepare the Broth:**
    - In a saucepan, heat the chicken or vegetable broth over low heat. Keep it warm throughout the cooking process.
2. **Sauté the Mushrooms:**
    - In a large skillet or sauté pan, heat 1 tablespoon of olive oil over medium-high heat. Add the sliced wild mushrooms and cook until they are golden brown and tender, about 5-7 minutes. Remove the mushrooms from the pan and set them aside.
3. **Cook the Aromatics:**
    - In a large, heavy-bottomed pot or Dutch oven, heat the remaining 1 tablespoon of olive oil and 1 tablespoon of butter over medium heat. Add the chopped onion and cook until it becomes translucent, about 3-4 minutes. Add the minced garlic and cook for an additional 1 minute.
4. **Toast the Rice:**
    - Add the Arborio rice to the pot and cook, stirring constantly, for 1-2 minutes until the rice is lightly toasted and coated with the oil and butter.
5. **Deglaze with Wine:**
    - Pour in the white wine and stir until it has mostly evaporated.
6. **Add the Broth:**
    - Begin adding the warm broth to the rice, one ladleful at a time. Stir frequently, allowing each addition of broth to be absorbed before adding the next. Continue this process until the rice is creamy and cooked to al dente, about 18-20 minutes.
7. **Combine Ingredients:**
    - When the rice is almost done, stir in the sautéed mushrooms. Cook for an additional 2-3 minutes, until the mushrooms are heated through and well incorporated.

8. **Finish the Risotto:**
    - Stir in the freshly grated Parmesan cheese and heavy cream (if using) until well combined. Adjust seasoning with salt and black pepper to taste.
9. **Garnish and Serve:**
    - Remove the pot from heat and stir in the chopped fresh parsley. Serve the risotto immediately, garnished with extra Parmesan cheese if desired.

Enjoy your creamy and flavorful Wild Mushroom Risotto!

Salmon with Lemon-Dill Sauce

Ingredients:

For the Salmon:

- 4 salmon fillets (6 oz each), skinless
- 2 tablespoons olive oil
- Salt and black pepper to taste
- 1 lemon, sliced (for garnish)

For the Lemon-Dill Sauce:

- 1 cup sour cream or Greek yogurt
- 2 tablespoons mayonnaise
- 1 tablespoon fresh dill, chopped (or 1 teaspoon dried dill)
- 1 tablespoon fresh lemon juice
- 1 teaspoon lemon zest
- 1 clove garlic, minced
- Salt and black pepper to taste

Instructions:

1. **Prepare the Sauce:**
    - In a medium bowl, combine the sour cream (or Greek yogurt), mayonnaise, chopped dill, lemon juice, lemon zest, and minced garlic. Mix well.
    - Season the sauce with salt and black pepper to taste. Cover and refrigerate until ready to use.
2. **Prepare the Salmon:**
    - Preheat your oven to 400°F (200°C). Alternatively, you can grill the salmon.
    - Brush the salmon fillets with olive oil and season with salt and black pepper.
    - Place the fillets on a baking sheet lined with parchment paper or aluminum foil.
3. **Cook the Salmon:**
    - **Oven Method:** Bake the salmon in the preheated oven for 12-15 minutes, or until the salmon is cooked through and flakes easily with a fork.
    - **Grill Method:** Preheat the grill to medium-high heat. Grill the salmon for about 4-5 minutes per side, or until cooked through.
4. **Serve:**
    - Transfer the cooked salmon fillets to serving plates.
    - Spoon a generous amount of lemon-dill sauce over each fillet.
    - Garnish with lemon slices and additional fresh dill if desired.
5. **Optional Side:**
    - Serve with your favorite sides such as roasted vegetables, rice, or a fresh salad.

Enjoy your flavorful and creamy Salmon with Lemon-Dill Sauce!

Marionberry Pie

Ingredients:

For the Pie Crust:

- 2 1/2 cups all-purpose flour
- 1 teaspoon granulated sugar
- 1 teaspoon salt
- 1 cup (2 sticks) unsalted butter, chilled and cut into small pieces
- 6-8 tablespoons ice water

For the Filling:

- 5 cups fresh or frozen marionberries
- 1 cup granulated sugar
- 1/4 cup cornstarch
- 1 tablespoon lemon juice
- 1/2 teaspoon lemon zest
- 1/4 teaspoon ground cinnamon (optional)
- 1/4 teaspoon salt
- 1 tablespoon unsalted butter, cut into small pieces (for dotting)

For Assembly:

- 1 egg, beaten (for egg wash)
- 1 tablespoon granulated sugar (for sprinkling)

Instructions:

1. **Prepare the Pie Crust:**
    - In a large bowl, whisk together the flour, sugar, and salt.
    - Add the chilled butter pieces and use a pastry cutter or your fingers to work the butter into the flour until the mixture resembles coarse crumbs.
    - Gradually add ice water, one tablespoon at a time, mixing until the dough just comes together. It should be moist but not sticky.
    - Divide the dough in half, shape each half into a disc, wrap in plastic wrap, and refrigerate for at least 1 hour.
2. **Prepare the Filling:**
    - In a large bowl, gently toss the marionberries with sugar, cornstarch, lemon juice, lemon zest, cinnamon (if using), and salt. Set aside to allow the berries to release their juices.
3. **Assemble the Pie:**
    - Preheat your oven to 375°F (190°C).
    - On a lightly floured surface, roll out one disc of dough into a circle about 12 inches in diameter. Transfer it to a 9-inch pie dish, trimming any excess dough.

- - Pour the berry mixture into the pie crust and dot with butter pieces.
  - Roll out the second disc of dough and place it over the filling. You can either use a full top crust or create a lattice pattern by cutting the dough into strips and weaving them over the filling.
  - Trim, fold, and crimp the edges of the crust to seal.
  - Brush the top crust with the beaten egg and sprinkle with granulated sugar for a nice finish.
4. **Bake the Pie:**
   - Place the pie on a baking sheet (to catch any drips) and bake in the preheated oven for 50-60 minutes, or until the crust is golden brown and the filling is bubbly. If the edges of the crust start to brown too quickly, cover them with foil to prevent burning.
5. **Cool and Serve:**
   - Allow the pie to cool completely on a wire rack before slicing. This will help the filling set.

Enjoy your homemade Marionberry Pie with a scoop of vanilla ice cream or a dollop of whipped cream!

Oregon Hazelnut Crusted Chicken

Ingredients:

- 4 boneless, skinless chicken breasts
- 1 cup raw hazelnuts
- 1 cup panko breadcrumbs
- 1/2 cup grated Parmesan cheese
- 1/2 teaspoon garlic powder
- 1/2 teaspoon onion powder
- 1/2 teaspoon dried thyme
- Salt and black pepper to taste
- 2 large eggs
- 2 tablespoons Dijon mustard
- 1/4 cup all-purpose flour
- 2 tablespoons olive oil (for cooking)

Instructions:

1. **Prepare the Hazelnuts:**
   - Preheat your oven to 350°F (175°C). Spread the raw hazelnuts on a baking sheet and toast in the oven for about 8-10 minutes, or until fragrant and lightly browned. Let them cool slightly.
   - Once cooled, pulse the hazelnuts in a food processor until finely chopped but not ground into a paste. Be careful not to over-process; you want a coarse crumb texture.
2. **Prepare the Crumb Mixture:**
   - In a shallow bowl, combine the chopped hazelnuts, panko breadcrumbs, Parmesan cheese, garlic powder, onion powder, dried thyme, salt, and black pepper. Mix well.
3. **Prepare the Chicken:**
   - Place the chicken breasts between two sheets of plastic wrap or parchment paper. Pound them with a meat mallet or rolling pin until they are an even thickness, about 1/2 inch thick.
   - Set up a breading station with three shallow dishes:
     - In the first dish, place the flour.
     - In the second dish, whisk together the eggs and Dijon mustard.
     - In the third dish, place the hazelnut breadcrumb mixture.
4. **Bread the Chicken:**
   - Dredge each chicken breast in the flour, shaking off excess.
   - Dip the chicken into the egg mixture, allowing any excess to drip off.
   - Coat the chicken with the hazelnut breadcrumb mixture, pressing gently to adhere.
5. **Cook the Chicken:**
   - Heat the olive oil in a large skillet over medium heat.

- Add the chicken breasts and cook for about 4-5 minutes per side, or until the crust is golden brown and the chicken is cooked through (internal temperature should reach 165°F or 74°C). If needed, you can finish cooking the chicken in a preheated oven at 350°F (175°C) for an additional 10 minutes.
6. **Serve:**
    - Remove the chicken from the skillet and let it rest for a few minutes before slicing.
    - Serve the chicken with your choice of sides, such as roasted vegetables, a fresh salad, or rice.

Enjoy your crispy and nutty Oregon Hazelnut Crusted Chicken!

Dungeness Crab Cakes

Ingredients:

- **For the Crab Cakes:**
    - 1 pound Dungeness crab meat, picked over for shells
    - ½ cup mayonnaise
    - 1 large egg, lightly beaten
    - 1 tablespoon Dijon mustard
    - 1 tablespoon fresh lemon juice
    - 1 tablespoon fresh parsley, chopped
    - ½ teaspoon Old Bay seasoning
    - ¼ teaspoon paprika
    - ¼ teaspoon garlic powder
    - ¼ teaspoon onion powder
    - 1 cup panko breadcrumbs
    - 2 tablespoons all-purpose flour
    - Salt and black pepper to taste
    - Vegetable oil for frying
- **For the Remoulade Sauce (optional):**
    - ½ cup mayonnaise
    - 2 tablespoons Dijon mustard
    - 1 tablespoon fresh lemon juice
    - 1 tablespoon fresh parsley, chopped
    - 1 teaspoon hot sauce (adjust to taste)
    - 1 teaspoon capers, chopped (optional)
    - 1 clove garlic, minced
    - Salt and pepper to taste

Instructions:

1. **Prepare the Crab Cake Mixture:**
    - In a large bowl, combine the mayonnaise, beaten egg, Dijon mustard, lemon juice, chopped parsley, Old Bay seasoning, paprika, garlic powder, and onion powder. Mix well.
    - Gently fold in the Dungeness crab meat, being careful not to break up the crab too much.
    - Gradually add the panko breadcrumbs and flour, mixing gently until just combined. Season with salt and black pepper to taste.
    - Refrigerate the crab cake mixture for at least 30 minutes to help the cakes hold together better.
2. **Form the Crab Cakes:**
    - Shape the crab mixture into 8-10 patties, about 1 inch thick. You can use your hands or a cookie cutter to help shape them.

3. **Cook the Crab Cakes:**
    - Heat a few tablespoons of vegetable oil in a large skillet over medium heat.
    - Add the crab cakes to the skillet, working in batches if necessary to avoid overcrowding.
    - Cook for 3-4 minutes per side, or until golden brown and crispy. The cakes should be heated through and have a nice crispy exterior.
4. **Prepare the Remoulade Sauce (optional):**
    - In a small bowl, whisk together the mayonnaise, Dijon mustard, lemon juice, chopped parsley, hot sauce, capers (if using), minced garlic, salt, and pepper.
    - Adjust seasoning to taste.
5. **Serve:**
    - Serve the crab cakes warm with the remoulade sauce on the side, if desired.

Tips:

- **For Extra Flavor:** Add a bit of finely chopped green onions or bell peppers to the crab mixture.
- **For a More Delicate Cake:** Use less panko breadcrumbs or substitute with crushed Ritz crackers for a more tender texture.
- **For Crispy Cakes:** Ensure the oil is hot before adding the crab cakes to get a nice crisp crust.

Enjoy your Dungeness Crab Cakes, a delicious and sophisticated dish that's sure to impress!

Pear and Hazelnut Salad

Ingredients:

- **For the Salad:**
    - 4 cups mixed greens (such as arugula, spinach, or baby kale)
    - 2 ripe pears, cored and sliced (Bartlett or Anjou pears work well)
    - ½ cup toasted hazelnuts, roughly chopped
    - ¼ cup crumbled goat cheese or feta cheese
    - ¼ cup thinly sliced red onion
    - ¼ cup dried cranberries or pomegranate seeds (optional)
    - 2 tablespoons fresh parsley, chopped (for garnish)
- **For the Vinaigrette:**
    - 3 tablespoons extra-virgin olive oil
    - 2 tablespoons balsamic vinegar (or apple cider vinegar)
    - 1 tablespoon honey or maple syrup
    - 1 teaspoon Dijon mustard
    - 1 clove garlic, minced
    - Salt and black pepper to taste

Instructions:

1. **Prepare the Vinaigrette:**
    - In a small bowl or jar, whisk together the olive oil, balsamic vinegar, honey or maple syrup, Dijon mustard, minced garlic, salt, and black pepper until well combined. Adjust seasoning to taste.
2. **Prepare the Salad Ingredients:**
    - In a large salad bowl, combine the mixed greens, sliced pears, toasted hazelnuts, crumbled goat cheese or feta cheese, and thinly sliced red onion.
    - If using dried cranberries or pomegranate seeds, add them to the bowl as well.
3. **Assemble the Salad:**
    - Drizzle the vinaigrette over the salad just before serving. Toss gently to coat the ingredients evenly.
    - Garnish with chopped fresh parsley.
4. **Serve:**
    - Serve immediately, or keep the salad components separate until ready to serve to maintain the freshness of the greens.

Tips:

- **For Extra Flavor:** Add a few thin slices of fresh apple or some roasted beets for additional sweetness and texture.
- **For a Crunchy Topping:** Consider adding a handful of candied nuts or croutons for extra crunch.

- **For a Make-Ahead Option:** Prepare the vinaigrette and chop the vegetables ahead of time, but assemble the salad just before serving to keep the greens crisp.

Enjoy your Pear and Hazelnut Salad, a perfect blend of sweet, savory, and crunchy flavors!

Oregon Wine-Braised Short Ribs

Ingredients:

- **For the Short Ribs:**
    - 4 pounds beef short ribs (about 8 pieces)
    - Salt and black pepper to taste
    - 2 tablespoons vegetable oil
    - 1 large onion, chopped
    - 2 carrots, peeled and chopped
    - 2 celery stalks, chopped
    - 4 cloves garlic, minced
    - 2 tablespoons tomato paste
    - 2 cups Oregon red wine (or any full-bodied red wine)
    - 2 cups beef broth
    - 1 cup diced canned tomatoes (or fresh, peeled and chopped)
    - 2 bay leaves
    - 1 teaspoon dried thyme
    - 1 teaspoon dried rosemary
    - 1 tablespoon Worcestershire sauce
- **For Garnish:**
    - Fresh parsley, chopped (optional)

Instructions:

1. **Prepare the Short Ribs:**
    - Preheat your oven to 325°F (163°C).
    - Season the short ribs generously with salt and black pepper.
    - In a large, oven-safe Dutch oven or heavy-bottomed pot, heat the vegetable oil over medium-high heat.
    - Add the short ribs in batches, searing on all sides until browned. Transfer the browned short ribs to a plate and set aside.
2. **Prepare the Vegetables:**
    - In the same pot, add the chopped onion, carrots, and celery. Cook, stirring occasionally, until the vegetables are softened, about 5-7 minutes.
    - Add the minced garlic and cook for an additional minute.
    - Stir in the tomato paste and cook for 2 minutes, allowing it to caramelize slightly.
3. **Deglaze and Braise:**
    - Pour in the red wine, scraping up any browned bits from the bottom of the pot with a wooden spoon.
    - Bring the wine to a boil and let it reduce by half, about 10 minutes.
    - Add the beef broth, diced tomatoes, bay leaves, dried thyme, dried rosemary, and Worcestershire sauce. Stir to combine.

- Return the seared short ribs to the pot, making sure they are mostly submerged in the liquid.
4. **Braise the Short Ribs:**
    - Cover the pot with a lid and transfer it to the preheated oven.
    - Braise the short ribs for 2 ½ to 3 hours, or until the meat is tender and easily pulls away from the bone.
5. **Finish and Serve:**
    - Remove the pot from the oven and let it cool slightly. Discard the bay leaves.
    - Skim any excess fat from the surface of the sauce. If you'd like a thicker sauce, you can simmer it on the stovetop over medium heat until reduced to your desired consistency.
    - Serve the short ribs with the sauce spooned over the top, and garnish with fresh parsley if desired.

Tips:

- **For Extra Flavor:** Consider adding a few sprigs of fresh thyme or rosemary to the pot during the braising process.
- **For a Complete Meal:** Serve the short ribs with mashed potatoes, polenta, or a side of roasted vegetables to soak up the delicious sauce.

Enjoy your Oregon Wine-Braised Short Ribs, a rich and flavorful dish that's sure to impress!

Raspberry-Glazed Pork Chops

Ingredients:

- **For the Pork Chops:**
    - 4 bone-in or boneless pork chops (about 1 inch thick)
    - Salt and black pepper to taste
    - 1 tablespoon olive oil
- **For the Raspberry Glaze:**
    - 1 cup fresh or frozen raspberries (thawed if frozen)
    - ¼ cup granulated sugar
    - 2 tablespoons balsamic vinegar
    - 1 tablespoon Dijon mustard
    - 1 teaspoon fresh thyme leaves (or ½ teaspoon dried thyme)
    - 1 teaspoon cornstarch (optional, for thickening)
    - 1 tablespoon water (if using cornstarch)

Instructions:

1. **Prepare the Raspberry Glaze:**
    - In a small saucepan, combine the raspberries, sugar, balsamic vinegar, Dijon mustard, and thyme.
    - Bring the mixture to a boil over medium heat, stirring frequently.
    - Reduce the heat and simmer for about 10 minutes, or until the raspberries break down and the glaze thickens slightly.
    - For a thicker glaze, dissolve the cornstarch in the tablespoon of water and stir it into the glaze. Cook for an additional 2 minutes, or until thickened to your liking.
    - Remove from heat and set aside.
2. **Prepare the Pork Chops:**
    - Season the pork chops with salt and black pepper on both sides.
    - Heat the olive oil in a large skillet over medium-high heat.
    - Add the pork chops to the skillet and cook for 5-7 minutes per side, or until they are cooked through and have an internal temperature of 145°F (63°C). The pork chops should be golden brown and slightly crispy on the outside.
    - Remove the pork chops from the skillet and let them rest on a plate for a few minutes.
3. **Glaze the Pork Chops:**
    - Return the skillet to medium heat.
    - Pour the raspberry glaze over the pork chops in the skillet, allowing it to warm and slightly caramelize around the chops.
    - Spoon some of the glaze over the pork chops, making sure they are well-coated.
4. **Serve:**
    - Serve the pork chops with additional raspberry glaze drizzled over the top.
    - Garnish with extra fresh thyme if desired.

Tips:

- **For Extra Flavor:** Add a splash of white wine or chicken broth to the glaze while simmering for a more complex taste.
- **For a Complete Meal:** Pair the pork chops with a side of roasted vegetables, rice, or a light salad to balance the richness of the glaze.

Enjoy your Raspberry-Glazed Pork Chops, a sweet and savory dish that's sure to impress your family and friends!

Smoked Trout Spread

Ingredients:

- **For the Spread:**
    - 8 ounces smoked trout, skin and bones removed
    - 4 ounces cream cheese, softened
    - ½ cup sour cream
    - 2 tablespoons fresh lemon juice
    - 1 tablespoon chopped fresh dill (or 1 teaspoon dried dill)
    - 1 tablespoon capers, drained and chopped
    - 1 small shallot, finely chopped
    - 1 tablespoon Dijon mustard
    - Salt and black pepper to taste
    - 1-2 teaspoons hot sauce (optional, for a bit of heat)
- **For Garnish (optional):**
    - Fresh dill sprigs
    - Lemon wedges
    - Sliced green onions

Instructions:

1. **Prepare the Ingredients:**
    - In a bowl, flake the smoked trout with a fork, ensuring no skin or bones remain.
2. **Combine the Spread:**
    - In a large mixing bowl, combine the cream cheese, sour cream, and lemon juice. Mix until smooth and well combined.
    - Add the flaked smoked trout, chopped fresh dill, capers, shallot, Dijon mustard, salt, black pepper, and hot sauce (if using). Gently fold the ingredients together until well incorporated.
3. **Adjust Seasoning:**
    - Taste the spread and adjust seasoning as needed with additional salt, black pepper, or hot sauce.
4. **Chill the Spread:**
    - Cover the bowl with plastic wrap or transfer the spread to an airtight container.
    - Refrigerate for at least 1 hour to allow the flavors to meld and the spread to firm up.
5. **Serve:**
    - Transfer the chilled spread to a serving dish.
    - Garnish with fresh dill sprigs, lemon wedges, and sliced green onions if desired.
    - Serve with crackers, toasted baguette slices, or fresh vegetable sticks.

Tips:

- **For a Creamier Texture:** Blend the cream cheese and sour cream together before mixing in the other ingredients.
- **For Added Flavor:** Incorporate finely chopped chives or a dash of smoked paprika for extra depth of flavor.
- **For a Smokier Taste:** Use smoked salmon if smoked trout is unavailable or if you prefer a stronger smoky flavor.

Enjoy your Smoked Trout Spread, a delicious and elegant appetizer that's sure to be a hit at your next gathering!

Huckleberry Pancakes

Ingredients:

- **For the Pancakes:**
    - 1 ½ cups all-purpose flour
    - 2 tablespoons granulated sugar
    - 1 tablespoon baking powder
    - ½ teaspoon baking soda
    - ¼ teaspoon salt
    - 1 cup buttermilk
    - 2 large eggs
    - 4 tablespoons unsalted butter, melted and slightly cooled
    - 1 cup fresh or frozen huckleberries (if using frozen, do not thaw)
- **For Serving:**
    - Maple syrup or honey
    - Fresh huckleberries (optional, for garnish)
    - Powdered sugar (optional, for garnish)

Instructions:

1. **Prepare the Pancake Batter:**
    - In a large bowl, whisk together the flour, sugar, baking powder, baking soda, and salt.
    - In a separate bowl, whisk together the buttermilk, eggs, and melted butter.
    - Pour the wet ingredients into the dry ingredients and gently stir until just combined. The batter will be lumpy; do not overmix.
    - Gently fold in the huckleberries.
2. **Cook the Pancakes:**
    - Heat a non-stick skillet or griddle over medium heat. Lightly grease with butter or cooking spray.
    - Pour about ¼ cup of batter onto the skillet for each pancake.
    - Cook until bubbles form on the surface and the edges look set, about 2-3 minutes.
    - Flip the pancakes and cook for an additional 1-2 minutes, or until golden brown and cooked through.
    - Keep the cooked pancakes warm in a low oven or covered with a clean towel while you cook the remaining pancakes.
3. **Serve:**
    - Serve the pancakes warm with maple syrup or honey.
    - Garnish with fresh huckleberries and a dusting of powdered sugar if desired.

Tips:

- **For Extra Fluffiness:** Let the batter rest for about 5 minutes before cooking to allow the baking powder to work its magic.
- **For Even Cooking:** Use a measuring cup to pour consistent amounts of batter onto the skillet for evenly sized pancakes.
- **For a Different Twist:** Add a teaspoon of vanilla extract or a sprinkle of cinnamon to the batter for additional flavor.

Enjoy your Huckleberry Pancakes, a sweet and flavorful breakfast treat that's sure to brighten your morning!

Oregon-style Beef Stroganoff

Ingredients:

- **For the Beef Stroganoff:**
    - 1 ½ pounds beef sirloin or tenderloin, sliced into thin strips
    - Salt and black pepper to taste
    - 2 tablespoons olive oil
    - 1 large onion, finely chopped
    - 3 cloves garlic, minced
    - 8 ounces cremini or button mushrooms, sliced
    - 1 tablespoon all-purpose flour
    - 1 cup Oregon red wine (or any dry red wine)
    - 1 cup beef broth
    - 1 tablespoon Worcestershire sauce
    - 1 teaspoon Dijon mustard
    - 1 teaspoon fresh thyme leaves (or ½ teaspoon dried thyme)
    - 1 cup sour cream
    - 2 tablespoons chopped fresh parsley (for garnish)
- **For Serving:**
    - Egg noodles, rice, or mashed potatoes

Instructions:

1. **Prepare the Beef:**
    - Season the beef strips with salt and black pepper.
    - Heat olive oil in a large skillet or Dutch oven over medium-high heat.
    - Add the beef strips and cook until browned on all sides, about 3-4 minutes. Remove the beef from the skillet and set aside.
2. **Cook the Vegetables:**
    - In the same skillet, add the chopped onion and cook until softened, about 5 minutes.
    - Add the minced garlic and sliced mushrooms. Cook until the mushrooms are tender and have released their juices, about 5-7 minutes.
3. **Make the Sauce:**
    - Stir in the flour and cook for 1-2 minutes to form a roux, which will help thicken the sauce.
    - Gradually pour in the red wine, scraping up any browned bits from the bottom of the skillet. Bring to a simmer and cook for 5 minutes, allowing the wine to reduce slightly.
    - Add the beef broth, Worcestershire sauce, Dijon mustard, and thyme. Stir to combine and bring to a simmer.
4. **Combine and Simmer:**

- Return the browned beef strips to the skillet, along with any juices that have accumulated.
- Reduce the heat to low and simmer for 10-15 minutes, or until the beef is cooked through and tender, and the sauce has thickened.

5. **Finish the Dish:**
   - Stir in the sour cream and cook for an additional 2-3 minutes, just until heated through. Do not boil after adding the sour cream to prevent curdling.

6. **Serve:**
   - Serve the beef stroganoff over egg noodles, rice, or mashed potatoes.
   - Garnish with chopped fresh parsley.

Tips:

- **For Extra Flavor:** Consider adding a splash of sherry or a teaspoon of Dijon mustard to the sauce for additional depth.
- **For a Creamier Texture:** Use full-fat sour cream or add a bit of heavy cream along with the sour cream.
- **For a More Earthy Flavor:** Incorporate additional mushrooms or use a mix of wild mushrooms if available.

Enjoy your Oregon-style Beef Stroganoff, a rich and satisfying dish that's perfect for a cozy meal!

Black Cod with Miso

Ingredients:

- **For the Miso Marinade:**
    - ¼ cup white miso paste
    - ¼ cup mirin (Japanese sweet rice wine)
    - ¼ cup sake (Japanese rice wine)
    - 2 tablespoons granulated sugar
    - 1 tablespoon soy sauce
    - 2 teaspoons freshly grated ginger
    - 2 cloves garlic, minced
- **For the Black Cod:**
    - 4 black cod fillets (about 6-8 ounces each)
    - Cooking spray or a light brush of oil
- **For Garnish (optional):**
    - Sliced green onions
    - Sesame seeds
    - Lemon wedges or lime wedges

Instructions:

1. **Prepare the Miso Marinade:**
    - In a bowl, whisk together the miso paste, mirin, sake, sugar, soy sauce, grated ginger, and minced garlic until smooth and well combined.
2. **Marinate the Black Cod:**
    - Pat the black cod fillets dry with paper towels.
    - Place the fillets in a large resealable plastic bag or shallow dish.
    - Pour the miso marinade over the fillets, ensuring they are well coated.
    - Seal the bag or cover the dish and refrigerate for at least 1 hour, or up to 24 hours for more intense flavor.
3. **Prepare to Cook:**
    - Preheat your broiler to high. Place an oven rack about 6 inches from the heat source.
    - Line a baking sheet with aluminum foil and lightly grease it with cooking spray or a brush of oil to prevent sticking.
4. **Broil the Black Cod:**
    - Remove the fillets from the marinade and gently wipe off excess marinade with a paper towel (to avoid burning during broiling).
    - Place the fillets on the prepared baking sheet.
    - Broil the black cod for 6-8 minutes, or until the fish is opaque and flakes easily with a fork. The surface should be caramelized and slightly charred.
5. **Serve:**
    - Transfer the broiled black cod to serving plates.

- Garnish with sliced green onions, sesame seeds, and lemon or lime wedges if desired.
- Serve with steamed rice and your choice of vegetables.

Tips:

- **For Extra Flavor:** Add a splash of rice vinegar to the marinade for a bit of acidity.
- **For a Crispy Finish:** If you prefer a crisper surface, broil the fish for an additional minute or two, but watch carefully to avoid burning.
- **For an Alternative Cooking Method:** You can also bake the marinated black cod at 375°F (190°C) for 15-20 minutes if you prefer not to broil.

Enjoy your Black Cod with Miso, a delicious and elegant dish that's perfect for a special occasion or a refined weeknight meal!

Grilled Salmon with Teriyaki Sauce

Ingredients:

- **For the Teriyaki Sauce:**
    - ¼ cup soy sauce
    - ¼ cup mirin (Japanese sweet rice wine)
    - 2 tablespoons honey or brown sugar
    - 2 tablespoons rice vinegar
    - 1 tablespoon freshly grated ginger
    - 1 garlic clove, minced
    - 1 teaspoon cornstarch mixed with 1 tablespoon water (optional, for thickening)
- **For the Salmon:**
    - 4 salmon fillets (about 6 ounces each)
    - Salt and black pepper to taste
    - 1 tablespoon olive oil
- **For Garnish (optional):**
    - Sliced green onions
    - Sesame seeds
    - Lemon or lime wedges
    - Fresh cilantro or parsley

Instructions:

1. **Prepare the Teriyaki Sauce:**
    - In a small saucepan, combine the soy sauce, mirin, honey or brown sugar, rice vinegar, grated ginger, and minced garlic.
    - Bring the mixture to a boil over medium heat, stirring occasionally.
    - Reduce the heat and let it simmer for 5-7 minutes, or until slightly reduced and thickened. If you prefer a thicker sauce, mix the cornstarch with water and stir it into the sauce. Cook for an additional 1-2 minutes until thickened.
    - Remove from heat and let cool. Reserve some sauce for serving and brush the rest on the salmon.
2. **Prepare the Salmon:**
    - Preheat your grill to medium-high heat (about 375-400°F or 190-200°C).
    - Pat the salmon fillets dry with paper towels and season both sides with salt and black pepper.
    - Brush the grill grates with olive oil to prevent sticking.
3. **Grill the Salmon:**
    - Place the salmon fillets skin-side down on the grill.
    - Grill for 4-5 minutes per side, or until the salmon is cooked through and flakes easily with a fork. The cooking time may vary depending on the thickness of the fillets.

- During the last few minutes of grilling, brush the salmon with the prepared teriyaki sauce.
4. **Serve:**
    - Transfer the grilled salmon to serving plates.
    - Drizzle with the reserved teriyaki sauce.
    - Garnish with sliced green onions, sesame seeds, and lemon or lime wedges if desired.
    - Serve with steamed rice, grilled vegetables, or a fresh salad.

Tips:

- **For Extra Flavor:** Marinate the salmon fillets in a small amount of the teriyaki sauce for 30 minutes before grilling.
- **For Grilled Vegetables:** Brush vegetables like bell peppers, zucchini, and asparagus with a bit of olive oil and grill alongside the salmon.
- **For a Different Twist:** Add a splash of lime juice or a sprinkle of chili flakes to the teriyaki sauce for added complexity and heat.

Enjoy your Grilled Salmon with Teriyaki Sauce, a tasty and easy-to-make dish that's sure to be a hit at your next meal!

Oregon Pinot Noir Beef Stew

Ingredients:

- **For the Stew:**
    - 2 pounds beef chuck, cut into 1-inch cubes
    - Salt and black pepper to taste
    - 3 tablespoons olive oil
    - 1 large onion, chopped
    - 3 cloves garlic, minced
    - 4 medium carrots, peeled and sliced
    - 3 celery stalks, chopped
    - 2 tablespoons tomato paste
    - 1 cup Oregon Pinot Noir (or any good-quality red wine)
    - 2 cups beef broth
    - 1 cup low-sodium chicken broth (or additional beef broth)
    - 2 bay leaves
    - 1 teaspoon dried thyme
    - 1 teaspoon dried rosemary
    - 1 tablespoon Worcestershire sauce
    - 1 cup frozen peas
    - 2 tablespoons all-purpose flour (optional, for thickening)
- **For Garnish (optional):**
    - Fresh parsley, chopped

Instructions:

1. **Prepare the Beef:**
    - Season the beef cubes with salt and black pepper.
    - Heat 2 tablespoons of olive oil in a large Dutch oven or heavy-bottomed pot over medium-high heat.
    - Add the beef in batches, searing on all sides until browned. Transfer the browned beef to a plate and set aside.
2. **Cook the Vegetables:**
    - In the same pot, add the remaining 1 tablespoon of olive oil.
    - Add the chopped onion, carrots, and celery. Cook until the vegetables are softened, about 5-7 minutes.
    - Add the minced garlic and cook for an additional minute.
    - Stir in the tomato paste and cook for 2 minutes.
3. **Deglaze and Simmer:**
    - Pour in the Pinot Noir, scraping up any browned bits from the bottom of the pot with a wooden spoon. Bring the wine to a simmer and cook for 5 minutes.
    - Add the beef broth, chicken broth, bay leaves, dried thyme, dried rosemary, and Worcestershire sauce. Stir to combine.

- Return the seared beef and any accumulated juices to the pot.

4. **Braise the Stew:**
   - Bring the mixture to a boil, then reduce the heat to low.
   - Cover and simmer for 1 ½ to 2 hours, or until the beef is tender and the flavors are well combined.

5. **Finish the Stew:**
   - Add the frozen peas and cook for an additional 5-10 minutes.
   - If you prefer a thicker stew, mix 2 tablespoons of flour with a small amount of water to form a slurry. Stir the slurry into the stew and cook for an additional 5 minutes, until the stew has thickened.

6. **Serve:**
   - Remove the bay leaves from the stew.
   - Serve hot, garnished with chopped fresh parsley if desired.
   - Enjoy with crusty bread, over mashed potatoes, or alongside steamed rice.

Tips:

- **For Extra Flavor:** Consider adding a splash of balsamic vinegar or a teaspoon of Dijon mustard to the stew for added depth.
- **For a Richer Stew:** Use beef broth made from scratch or a high-quality store-bought variety for a richer flavor.
- **For a Lighter Option:** Substitute some of the beef broth with water to reduce the richness.

Enjoy your Oregon Pinot Noir Beef Stew, a hearty and flavorful dish that brings the essence of Oregon's wine country right to your table!

Chanterelle Mushroom Soup

Ingredients:

- **For the Soup:**
    - 1 tablespoon olive oil
    - 1 medium onion, chopped
    - 3 cloves garlic, minced
    - 1 pound chanterelle mushrooms, cleaned and sliced
    - 1 teaspoon fresh thyme leaves (or ½ teaspoon dried thyme)
    - 4 cups vegetable broth or chicken broth
    - 1 cup heavy cream
    - 2 tablespoons all-purpose flour (optional, for thickening)
    - Salt and black pepper to taste
- **For Garnish (optional):**
    - Chopped fresh parsley
    - Sliced chanterelle mushrooms (sautéed)
    - A drizzle of truffle oil (optional)

Instructions:

1. **Prepare the Ingredients:**
    - Clean and slice the chanterelle mushrooms. If using dried mushrooms, soak them in warm water for 20-30 minutes and then slice.
2. **Cook the Vegetables:**
    - Heat the olive oil in a large pot over medium heat.
    - Add the chopped onion and cook until softened and translucent, about 5 minutes.
    - Add the minced garlic and cook for an additional 1 minute.
3. **Sauté the Mushrooms:**
    - Add the sliced chanterelle mushrooms to the pot. Cook, stirring occasionally, until the mushrooms are tender and have released their moisture, about 8-10 minutes.
    - Stir in the fresh thyme and cook for 1 more minute.
4. **Add Broth and Simmer:**
    - Pour in the vegetable broth or chicken broth, stirring to combine.
    - Bring the mixture to a boil, then reduce the heat and let it simmer for 10-15 minutes to allow the flavors to meld.
5. **Blend the Soup:**
    - Using an immersion blender, carefully blend the soup until smooth. Alternatively, you can blend the soup in batches using a regular blender. If you prefer a chunkier texture, blend only half of the soup.
    - Return the blended soup to the pot.
6. **Finish the Soup:**
    - Stir in the heavy cream and cook for an additional 5 minutes. If you prefer a thicker soup, mix 2 tablespoons of flour with a small amount of water to form a

slurry and stir it into the soup. Cook for an additional 5 minutes, or until thickened.
- Season with salt and black pepper to taste.
7. **Serve:**
    - Ladle the soup into bowls.
    - Garnish with chopped fresh parsley, sautéed chanterelle mushroom slices, and a drizzle of truffle oil if desired.

Tips:

- **For Extra Flavor:** Consider adding a splash of white wine or a squeeze of lemon juice to the soup for added depth.
- **For a Creamier Texture:** Use half-and-half or milk instead of heavy cream, or add a bit of cream cheese.
- **For a Garnish:** Sauté extra chanterelle mushrooms in a bit of butter and use them as a garnish for added texture and flavor.

Enjoy your Chanterelle Mushroom Soup, a rich and comforting dish that showcases the unique flavors of chanterelle mushrooms!

Blackberry Sage Sorbet

Ingredients:

- **For the Sorbet:**
    - 4 cups fresh blackberries (or thawed frozen blackberries)
    - 1 cup granulated sugar
    - 1 cup water
    - 2 tablespoons freshly squeezed lemon juice
    - 1 tablespoon finely chopped fresh sage leaves (or 1 teaspoon dried sage)
    - 1 egg white (optional, for a smoother texture)

Instructions:

1. **Prepare the Blackberry Mixture:**
    - In a medium saucepan, combine the sugar and water. Heat over medium heat, stirring occasionally, until the sugar is completely dissolved. This creates a simple syrup. Remove from heat and let it cool to room temperature.
    - If using fresh blackberries, rinse them and remove any stems. If using frozen, ensure they are fully thawed and drained.
2. **Blend the Blackberries:**
    - In a blender or food processor, combine the blackberries and the cooled simple syrup. Blend until smooth.
    - Strain the blackberry mixture through a fine mesh sieve or cheesecloth into a large bowl to remove seeds and any pulp.
3. **Add Lemon Juice and Sage:**
    - Stir in the freshly squeezed lemon juice.
    - Add the finely chopped fresh sage leaves and mix well.
4. **Incorporate Egg White (Optional):**
    - For a smoother texture, lightly beat the egg white until frothy and fold it into the blackberry mixture. This step is optional and can be omitted if you prefer not to use egg white.
5. **Chill the Mixture:**
    - Chill the blackberry mixture in the refrigerator for at least 1 hour, or until it is thoroughly chilled. This helps the sorbet freeze more evenly.
6. **Freeze the Sorbet:**
    - Pour the chilled mixture into an ice cream maker and churn according to the manufacturer's instructions until it reaches a soft-serve consistency.
    - Transfer the sorbet to an airtight container and freeze for at least 2 hours to firm up.
7. **Serve:**
    - Scoop the sorbet into bowls or cones.
    - Garnish with additional sage leaves or fresh blackberries if desired.

Tips:

- **For Extra Flavor:** You can experiment with adding a splash of balsamic vinegar or a pinch of sea salt to the mixture for added depth.
- **For a Smoother Texture:** If you don't have an ice cream maker, pour the mixture into a shallow dish, freeze it, and stir every 30 minutes with a fork until it's frozen and fluffy.
- **For a Herbal Twist:** Try using other herbs like basil or mint in place of sage for different flavor profiles.

Enjoy your Blackberry Sage Sorbet, a sophisticated and refreshing treat that's perfect for warm days or special occasions!

Grilled Asparagus with Lemon

Ingredients:

- 1 bunch of fresh asparagus (about 1 pound)
- 2 tablespoons olive oil
- 1 lemon, zested and juiced
- 2 cloves garlic, minced
- Salt and black pepper to taste
- 2 tablespoons grated Parmesan cheese (optional, for garnish)
- Lemon wedges (for serving, optional)

Instructions:

1. **Prepare the Asparagus:**
    - Rinse the asparagus under cold water and pat dry with paper towels.
    - Trim the tough ends of the asparagus. You can snap them off by bending each spear gently until it breaks, or use a knife to cut off the woody ends.
2. **Season the Asparagus:**
    - In a large bowl, toss the asparagus with olive oil, minced garlic, lemon zest, and lemon juice.
    - Season with salt and black pepper to taste.
3. **Preheat the Grill:**
    - Preheat your grill to medium-high heat (about 400°F or 200°C).
    - If using a gas grill, heat the burners to medium-high. If using a charcoal grill, let the coals burn until they are covered with gray ash.
4. **Grill the Asparagus:**
    - Place the asparagus spears directly on the grill grates or use a grill basket to prevent them from falling through the grates.
    - Grill the asparagus for 4-6 minutes, turning occasionally, until they are tender and have grill marks. The asparagus should be slightly charred but still crisp-tender.
5. **Serve:**
    - Transfer the grilled asparagus to a serving platter.
    - Optionally, sprinkle with grated Parmesan cheese for added flavor.
    - Garnish with additional lemon zest if desired and serve with lemon wedges on the side.

Tips:

- **For Even Grilling:** Try to keep the asparagus spears in a single layer and avoid overcrowding them on the grill.
- **For Extra Flavor:** You can add a sprinkle of red pepper flakes for a bit of heat or a drizzle of balsamic glaze for added complexity.

- **For a Quick Prep:** If you're short on time, you can also roast the asparagus in the oven at 425°F (220°C) for 15-20 minutes, tossing halfway through.

Enjoy your Grilled Asparagus with Lemon, a fresh and vibrant side dish that's sure to complement any meal!

Hazelnut-Crusted Salmon

Ingredients:

- **For the Salmon:**
    - 4 salmon fillets (about 6 ounces each)
    - Salt and black pepper to taste
    - 1 tablespoon olive oil
- **For the Hazelnut Crust:**
    - ½ cup finely chopped hazelnuts (toasting optional but enhances flavor)
    - ½ cup panko breadcrumbs
    - 2 tablespoons grated Parmesan cheese
    - 2 tablespoons fresh parsley, finely chopped
    - 1 teaspoon Dijon mustard
    - 1 tablespoon melted butter (or additional olive oil)
    - 1 garlic clove, minced (optional)
- **For Garnish (optional):**
    - Lemon wedges
    - Fresh parsley

Instructions:

1. **Prepare the Hazelnut Crust:**
    - Preheat your oven to 375°F (190°C).
    - In a bowl, combine the chopped hazelnuts, panko breadcrumbs, grated Parmesan cheese, fresh parsley, Dijon mustard, melted butter, and minced garlic if using. Mix until well combined.
2. **Prepare the Salmon:**
    - Pat the salmon fillets dry with paper towels.
    - Season both sides of the salmon fillets with salt and black pepper.
    - Brush each fillet lightly with olive oil to help the crust adhere.
3. **Apply the Hazelnut Crust:**
    - Press the hazelnut mixture onto the top of each salmon fillet, pressing down gently to ensure it sticks well.
4. **Cook the Salmon:**
    - Heat a large ovenproof skillet over medium-high heat and add a bit of olive oil.
    - Once the skillet is hot, add the salmon fillets, crust-side down, and cook for 2-3 minutes until the crust is golden brown.
    - Carefully transfer the skillet to the preheated oven and bake for 8-12 minutes, depending on the thickness of the fillets, until the salmon is cooked through and flakes easily with a fork.
5. **Serve:**
    - Transfer the salmon fillets to serving plates.
    - Garnish with lemon wedges and additional fresh parsley if desired.

Tips:

- **For Extra Flavor:** Toast the hazelnuts in a dry skillet over medium heat for a few minutes until fragrant before chopping them. This step enhances the nutty flavor.
- **For a Crispier Crust:** If you like a crunchier crust, broil the salmon for the last 1-2 minutes of cooking, but keep a close eye to prevent burning.
- **For a Light Side:** Serve with a fresh salad or steamed vegetables for a light and balanced meal.

Enjoy your Hazelnut-Crusted Salmon, a flavorful and elegant dish that's sure to impress!

Portlandia-Style Veggie Burger

Ingredients:

- **For the Veggie Patty:**
    - 1 cup cooked quinoa (about ½ cup dry quinoa)
    - 1 can (15 ounces) black beans, drained and rinsed
    - 1 cup grated carrots
    - 1 cup finely chopped mushrooms (such as cremini or button)
    - 1 small onion, finely chopped
    - 2 cloves garlic, minced
    - 1 egg (or flax egg for a vegan option)
    - ½ cup breadcrumbs (whole wheat or regular)
    - ¼ cup chopped fresh parsley or cilantro
    - 1 teaspoon ground cumin
    - 1 teaspoon smoked paprika
    - ½ teaspoon ground coriander
    - Salt and black pepper to taste
    - 2 tablespoons olive oil (for cooking)
- **For Serving:**
    - Burger buns (whole grain or your choice)
    - Lettuce leaves
    - Tomato slices
    - Red onion slices
    - Avocado slices
    - Pickles
    - Your favorite burger condiments (such as mustard, ketchup, or aioli)

Instructions:

1. **Prepare the Ingredients:**
    - Cook the quinoa according to package instructions and let it cool.
    - Preheat your oven to 375°F (190°C) if you plan to bake the patties.
2. **Make the Veggie Patty Mixture:**
    - In a large mixing bowl, mash the black beans with a fork or potato masher, leaving some chunks for texture.
    - Add the grated carrots, chopped mushrooms, onion, and garlic to the bowl.
    - Stir in the cooked quinoa, breadcrumbs, parsley or cilantro, egg (or flax egg), cumin, smoked paprika, coriander, salt, and black pepper. Mix until well combined. The mixture should be moist but hold together when shaped into patties. If it's too wet, add more breadcrumbs; if too dry, add a splash of water.
3. **Form and Cook the Patties:**
    - Divide the mixture into 4-6 portions and shape each portion into a patty.

- Heat olive oil in a large skillet over medium heat. Cook the patties for about 4-5 minutes on each side, or until golden brown and crispy on the outside.
- Alternatively, you can bake the patties: Place them on a baking sheet lined with parchment paper and bake for 25-30 minutes, flipping halfway through, until they are firm and golden brown.

4. **Assemble the Burgers:**
   - Toast the burger buns if desired.
   - Place each veggie patty on the bottom half of a bun.
   - Top with lettuce, tomato slices, red onion slices, avocado slices, and pickles.
   - Add your favorite condiments and top with the other half of the bun.

5. **Serve:**
   - Serve the veggie burgers immediately with your choice of side dishes, such as sweet potato fries, a fresh salad, or roasted vegetables.

Tips:

- **For a Vegan Option:** Use a flax egg instead of a regular egg. To make a flax egg, mix 1 tablespoon ground flaxseed with 3 tablespoons water and let it sit for a few minutes until it becomes gel-like.
- **For Extra Flavor:** Experiment with adding different spices or herbs to the patty mixture, such as chili powder, turmeric, or fresh basil.
- **For a Juicier Patty:** You can add a tablespoon of vegetable broth or a splash of soy sauce to the mixture for extra moisture and flavor.

Enjoy your Portlandia-Style Veggie Burger, a delicious and hearty option that captures the spirit of Portland's creative food scene!

Apple Cider Brined Pork Loin

Ingredients:

- **For the Brine:**
    - 2 cups apple cider
    - 1 cup water
    - ¼ cup kosher salt
    - ¼ cup brown sugar
    - 1 tablespoon whole black peppercorns
    - 3 cloves garlic, smashed
    - 1 tablespoon fresh rosemary leaves (or 1 teaspoon dried rosemary)
    - 1 tablespoon fresh thyme leaves (or 1 teaspoon dried thyme)
    - 1 bay leaf
- **For the Pork Loin:**
    - 1 (3-4 pounds) pork loin
    - 2 tablespoons olive oil
    - 2 teaspoons fresh rosemary, chopped
    - 2 teaspoons fresh thyme, chopped
    - Salt and black pepper to taste
- **For Optional Glaze (if desired):**
    - ¼ cup apple cider
    - 2 tablespoons honey
    - 1 tablespoon Dijon mustard

Instructions:

1. **Prepare the Brine:**
    - In a large saucepan, combine the apple cider, water, kosher salt, brown sugar, peppercorns, garlic, rosemary, thyme, and bay leaf.
    - Bring the mixture to a boil, stirring until the salt and sugar are dissolved.
    - Remove from heat and let the brine cool to room temperature.
2. **Brine the Pork Loin:**
    - Place the pork loin in a large resealable plastic bag or a container with a lid.
    - Pour the cooled brine over the pork, making sure it's fully submerged. If needed, add more water to cover the meat.
    - Seal the bag or cover the container and refrigerate for at least 6 hours or overnight for best results.
3. **Prepare for Roasting:**
    - Preheat your oven to 375°F (190°C).
    - Remove the pork loin from the brine and pat it dry with paper towels. Discard the brine.
    - Rub the pork loin with olive oil, and season with chopped rosemary, thyme, salt, and black pepper.

4. **Roast the Pork Loin:**
    - Place the pork loin on a rack in a roasting pan.
    - Roast in the preheated oven for 45-60 minutes, or until the internal temperature reaches 145°F (63°C). The exact cooking time will depend on the size of your pork loin.
    - If using a glaze, combine the apple cider, honey, and Dijon mustard in a small saucepan. Bring to a simmer over medium heat and cook until slightly thickened, about 5-7 minutes. Brush the glaze onto the pork loin during the last 15 minutes of roasting.
5. **Rest and Serve:**
    - Remove the pork loin from the oven and let it rest for 10-15 minutes before slicing. This allows the juices to redistribute and keeps the meat tender.
    - Slice and serve with your choice of side dishes, such as roasted vegetables, mashed potatoes, or a fresh salad.

Tips:

- **For Extra Moisture:** Consider using a meat thermometer to ensure the pork loin is perfectly cooked and stays juicy.
- **For More Flavor:** You can add additional herbs or spices to the brine or the pork rub to suit your taste preferences.
- **For a Complete Meal:** Serve the pork loin with a warm apple compote or a side of sautéed greens for a well-rounded meal.

Enjoy your Apple Cider Brined Pork Loin, a flavorful and succulent dish that's perfect for any special occasion!

Oregon Raspberry Balsamic Vinaigrette

Ingredients:

- **For the Vinaigrette:**
    - ½ cup fresh raspberries (or thawed frozen raspberries)
    - ¼ cup balsamic vinegar
    - ¼ cup extra-virgin olive oil
    - 1 tablespoon honey or maple syrup (adjust to taste for sweetness)
    - 1 teaspoon Dijon mustard
    - 1 small garlic clove, minced
    - Salt and black pepper to taste

Instructions:

1. **Prepare the Raspberries:**
    - If using fresh raspberries, rinse them gently and pat them dry. If using frozen raspberries, thaw them and drain any excess liquid.
2. **Blend the Ingredients:**
    - In a blender or food processor, combine the raspberries, balsamic vinegar, honey or maple syrup, Dijon mustard, and minced garlic. Blend until smooth.
3. **Emulsify the Vinaigrette:**
    - With the blender or food processor running, slowly drizzle in the olive oil until the vinaigrette is fully emulsified and creamy.
4. **Season and Adjust:**
    - Taste the vinaigrette and season with salt and black pepper to taste.
    - If the vinaigrette is too tart, add a little more honey or maple syrup. If it's too thick, you can thin it with a small amount of water or additional balsamic vinegar.
5. **Serve or Store:**
    - Transfer the vinaigrette to a jar or bottle with a tight-fitting lid.
    - Store in the refrigerator for up to 1 week. Shake well before each use as the ingredients may separate over time.

Tips:

- **For a Smoother Texture:** Strain the vinaigrette through a fine-mesh sieve to remove any raspberry seeds and achieve a smoother consistency.
- **For Extra Flavor:** Consider adding a pinch of dried herbs, such as thyme or basil, to the vinaigrette for additional depth of flavor.
- **For a Creamy Version:** You can add a tablespoon of Greek yogurt or mayonnaise to the vinaigrette to make it creamy.

Enjoy your Oregon Raspberry Balsamic Vinaigrette, a delicious and versatile dressing that brings a burst of fresh, fruity flavor to your dishes!

Roasted Beet and Goat Cheese Salad

Ingredients:

- **For the Salad:**
    - 4 medium beets, peeled and cut into wedges
    - 2 tablespoons olive oil
    - Salt and black pepper to taste
    - 4 cups mixed greens (such as arugula, spinach, and baby kale)
    - ½ cup crumbled goat cheese
    - ¼ cup chopped walnuts or pecans (toasted if desired)
    - 1 small red onion, thinly sliced
    - 1-2 tablespoons fresh chives or parsley, chopped (for garnish)
- **For the Vinaigrette:**
    - 3 tablespoons balsamic vinegar
    - 2 tablespoons extra-virgin olive oil
    - 1 teaspoon Dijon mustard
    - 1 teaspoon honey or maple syrup
    - 1 small garlic clove, minced
    - Salt and black pepper to taste

Instructions:

1. **Roast the Beets:**
    - Preheat your oven to 400°F (200°C).
    - Place the beet wedges on a baking sheet and drizzle with olive oil. Toss to coat and season with salt and black pepper.
    - Roast in the preheated oven for 30-40 minutes, or until the beets are tender and can be easily pierced with a fork. Stir once or twice during roasting for even cooking.
    - Allow the beets to cool slightly before handling.
2. **Prepare the Vinaigrette:**
    - In a small bowl or jar, whisk together the balsamic vinegar, olive oil, Dijon mustard, honey or maple syrup, minced garlic, salt, and black pepper until well combined. Adjust seasoning to taste.
3. **Assemble the Salad:**
    - In a large bowl, toss the mixed greens with a small amount of the vinaigrette to lightly coat them.
    - Arrange the dressed greens on a serving platter or individual plates.
    - Scatter the roasted beets over the greens.
    - Sprinkle the crumbled goat cheese, toasted walnuts or pecans, and thinly sliced red onion on top.
4. **Garnish and Serve:**
    - Drizzle the remaining vinaigrette over the salad, or serve it on the side.

- Garnish with chopped fresh chives or parsley if desired.
- Serve immediately.

Tips:

- **For Extra Flavor:** Add a sprinkle of sea salt or freshly cracked black pepper just before serving for added seasoning.
- **For Added Texture:** Consider adding some roasted chickpeas or croutons for an extra crunch.
- **For a Make-Ahead Option:** Roast the beets and prepare the vinaigrette a day ahead. Assemble the salad just before serving to keep the greens fresh.

Enjoy your Roasted Beet and Goat Cheese Salad, a vibrant and flavorful dish that's sure to impress!

Wild Salmon Teriyaki

Ingredients:

- **For the Salmon:**
    - 4 wild salmon fillets (about 6 ounces each)
    - Salt and black pepper to taste
    - 1 tablespoon olive oil or vegetable oil
- **For the Teriyaki Sauce:**
    - ¼ cup soy sauce
    - ¼ cup mirin (Japanese sweet rice wine)
    - 2 tablespoons honey or maple syrup
    - 2 tablespoons rice vinegar
    - 1 clove garlic, minced
    - 1 teaspoon freshly grated ginger
    - 1 tablespoon cornstarch mixed with 2 tablespoons water (for thickening, optional)
    - Sesame seeds (for garnish, optional)
    - Sliced green onions (for garnish, optional)

Instructions:

1. **Prepare the Teriyaki Sauce:**
    - In a small saucepan, combine the soy sauce, mirin, honey (or maple syrup), rice vinegar, minced garlic, and grated ginger.
    - Bring the mixture to a simmer over medium heat, stirring occasionally.
    - If you prefer a thicker sauce, mix the cornstarch with water to form a slurry and add it to the saucepan. Continue to simmer for a few minutes until the sauce thickens.
    - Remove the saucepan from heat and let the sauce cool slightly.
2. **Prepare the Salmon:**
    - Preheat your oven to 375°F (190°C) if you plan to bake the salmon.
    - Season the salmon fillets with salt and black pepper.
    - Heat the oil in a large ovenproof skillet over medium-high heat. Add the salmon fillets, skin-side down, and sear for about 2-3 minutes until the skin is crispy.
    - Flip the salmon fillets and pour some of the teriyaki sauce over the top.
3. **Cook the Salmon:**
    - Transfer the skillet to the preheated oven and bake for 8-12 minutes, depending on the thickness of the fillets, until the salmon is cooked through and flakes easily with a fork.
    - Alternatively, you can continue to cook the salmon on the stovetop by covering the skillet with a lid and simmering for 5-7 minutes until cooked through.
4. **Serve:**
    - Remove the salmon from the oven or stovetop and transfer to serving plates.

- - Drizzle additional teriyaki sauce over the salmon, and garnish with sesame seeds and sliced green onions if desired.
  - Serve with steamed rice, sautéed vegetables, or a fresh salad.

Tips:

- **For Extra Flavor:** Marinate the salmon fillets in some of the teriyaki sauce for 30 minutes before cooking.
- **For a Crispier Skin:** Ensure the skin is dry before searing, and avoid moving the fillets around in the pan until you flip them.
- **For a Low-Sodium Option:** Use low-sodium soy sauce to reduce the sodium content of the dish.

Enjoy your Wild Salmon Teriyaki, a flavorful and satisfying dish that brings together the best of savory and sweet!

Pumpkin Ale Bread

Ingredients:

- **For the Bread:**
    - 1 ½ cups all-purpose flour
    - 1 cup whole wheat flour
    - 1 tablespoon baking powder
    - 1 teaspoon baking soda
    - 1 teaspoon ground cinnamon
    - ½ teaspoon ground nutmeg
    - ½ teaspoon salt
    - 1 cup canned pumpkin (not pumpkin pie filling)
    - ½ cup pumpkin ale or a similar beer (or substitute with a non-alcoholic beer or apple cider)
    - ¼ cup honey or maple syrup
    - ¼ cup vegetable oil or melted butter
    - 2 large eggs
- **For Optional Topping:**
    - 2 tablespoons raw sugar or turbinado sugar
    - 1 teaspoon ground cinnamon

Instructions:

1. **Preheat the Oven:**
    - Preheat your oven to 350°F (175°C). Grease a 9x5-inch loaf pan or line it with parchment paper.
2. **Prepare the Dry Ingredients:**
    - In a large bowl, whisk together the all-purpose flour, whole wheat flour, baking powder, baking soda, ground cinnamon, ground nutmeg, and salt.
3. **Combine the Wet Ingredients:**
    - In another bowl, combine the canned pumpkin, pumpkin ale, honey or maple syrup, vegetable oil (or melted butter), and eggs. Mix well until smooth.
4. **Mix the Batter:**
    - Pour the wet ingredients into the dry ingredients and stir gently until just combined. Be careful not to overmix; it's okay if there are a few lumps.
5. **Pour into Pan:**
    - Transfer the batter to the prepared loaf pan and smooth the top with a spatula.
6. **Add Optional Topping:**
    - If desired, mix the raw sugar with ground cinnamon and sprinkle it over the top of the batter for a sweet, crunchy topping.
7. **Bake the Bread:**
    - Bake in the preheated oven for 50-60 minutes, or until a toothpick inserted into the center of the loaf comes out clean.

8. **Cool and Serve:**
    - Allow the bread to cool in the pan for about 10 minutes before transferring it to a wire rack to cool completely.
    - Slice and serve. This bread is great on its own or with a spread of butter or cream cheese.

Tips:

- **For Extra Moisture:** You can add ¼ cup of plain Greek yogurt or sour cream to the wet ingredients for a richer texture.
- **For a Spiced Variation:** Add a pinch of cloves or allspice to the dry ingredients for additional warmth.
- **For a Nutty Touch:** Fold in ½ cup of chopped walnuts or pecans into the batter before baking.

Enjoy your Pumpkin Ale Bread, a delightful and flavorful bread that combines the essence of autumn with a touch of beer's unique taste!

Oregon Blueberry Cheesecake

Ingredients:

- **For the Crust:**
    - 1 ½ cups graham cracker crumbs (about 12-14 graham crackers, crushed)
    - ¼ cup granulated sugar
    - 6 tablespoons unsalted butter, melted
- **For the Cheesecake Filling:**
    - 4 (8-ounce) packages cream cheese, softened
    - 1 cup granulated sugar
    - 1 teaspoon vanilla extract
    - 4 large eggs
    - 1 cup sour cream
    - 1 cup heavy cream
- **For the Blueberry Compote:**
    - 2 cups fresh or frozen blueberries
    - ¼ cup granulated sugar
    - 1 tablespoon lemon juice
    - 1 teaspoon cornstarch mixed with 1 tablespoon water (for thickening, optional)

Instructions:

1. **Prepare the Crust:**
    - Preheat your oven to 325°F (163°C).
    - In a medium bowl, combine the graham cracker crumbs, granulated sugar, and melted butter. Mix until the crumbs are evenly coated.
    - Press the mixture firmly into the bottom of a 9-inch springform pan to form an even layer. Use the back of a spoon or the bottom of a glass to press it down.
    - Bake the crust in the preheated oven for 10 minutes. Remove from the oven and let it cool while you prepare the filling.
2. **Prepare the Cheesecake Filling:**
    - In a large mixing bowl, beat the cream cheese with an electric mixer on medium speed until smooth and creamy.
    - Add the granulated sugar and vanilla extract, and continue to beat until well combined.
    - Add the eggs one at a time, beating well after each addition.
    - Mix in the sour cream and heavy cream until the batter is smooth and creamy.
    - Pour the cheesecake batter over the cooled crust in the springform pan.
3. **Bake the Cheesecake:**
    - Place the springform pan on a baking sheet to catch any drips.
    - Bake in the preheated oven for 55-65 minutes, or until the center is set and the edges are slightly puffed. The center may still have a slight jiggle.

- Turn off the oven and crack the oven door slightly. Let the cheesecake cool in the oven for 1 hour. This helps prevent cracking.
 - Remove the cheesecake from the oven and refrigerate for at least 4 hours or overnight to chill and set.
4. **Prepare the Blueberry Compote:**
 - In a medium saucepan, combine the blueberries, granulated sugar, and lemon juice.
 - Cook over medium heat, stirring occasionally, until the blueberries release their juices and the mixture begins to simmer.
 - If you prefer a thicker compote, stir in the cornstarch mixture and cook for an additional 1-2 minutes until the compote thickens.
 - Remove from heat and let it cool completely.
5. **Assemble and Serve:**
 - Once the cheesecake has chilled and set, spread the blueberry compote evenly over the top.
 - Release the sides of the springform pan and remove it.
 - Slice and serve the cheesecake chilled.

Tips:

- **For a Smoother Cheesecake:** Make sure the cream cheese is fully softened and mixed well to avoid lumps.
- **For a Subtle Flavor:** Add a teaspoon of lemon zest to the cheesecake batter for a hint of citrus.
- **For a Decorative Touch:** Garnish the cheesecake with fresh blueberries or a sprig of mint before serving.

Enjoy your Oregon Blueberry Cheesecake, a rich and fruity dessert that's sure to impress!

Spiced Apple Cider

Ingredients:

- **For the Cider:**
    - 1 gallon apple cider (or apple juice)
    - 1 orange, sliced
    - 4-6 whole cloves
    - 3-4 cinnamon sticks
    - 1 tablespoon whole allspice berries
    - 1 tablespoon whole peppercorns
    - 1-2 tablespoons brown sugar or maple syrup (to taste)
    - 1-2 tablespoons fresh lemon juice (optional, to taste)
- **For Garnish (Optional):**
    - Additional cinnamon sticks
    - Apple slices
    - Orange slices

Instructions:

1. **Prepare the Spices:**
    - In a large pot, combine the apple cider with the orange slices, cloves, cinnamon sticks, allspice berries, and peppercorns.
2. **Simmer the Cider:**
    - Heat the mixture over medium heat until it begins to simmer. Reduce the heat to low and let it simmer gently for 20-30 minutes to allow the flavors to meld together.
    - Taste the cider and stir in brown sugar or maple syrup to sweeten to your liking. You can also add lemon juice at this stage if you prefer a touch of tartness.
3. **Strain and Serve:**
    - Once the cider has finished simmering, remove the pot from the heat.
    - Strain the cider through a fine-mesh sieve or cheesecloth to remove the whole spices and orange slices.
4. **Garnish and Enjoy:**
    - Serve the cider hot in mugs or cups.
    - Garnish with additional cinnamon sticks and slices of apple or orange if desired.

Tips:

- **For a Richer Flavor:** You can add a splash of dark rum or bourbon to individual servings for an adult twist.
- **For a Non-Alcoholic Option:** Simply skip the alcohol and enjoy the cider as is or with a splash of sparkling water for a fizzy version.

- **For a Make-Ahead Option:** You can prepare the spiced cider a day in advance and reheat it before serving.

Enjoy your Spiced Apple Cider, a comforting and fragrant drink that brings the flavors of fall and winter right to your cup!

Pan-Seared Sea Bass with Herb Butter

Ingredients:

- **For the Sea Bass:**
    - 4 sea bass fillets (about 6 ounces each), skin-on or skinless
    - Salt and black pepper to taste
    - 2 tablespoons olive oil
- **For the Herb Butter:**
    - ½ cup unsalted butter, softened
    - 2 tablespoons fresh parsley, finely chopped
    - 1 tablespoon fresh chives, finely chopped
    - 1 tablespoon fresh dill, finely chopped (or use tarragon or basil)
    - 1 teaspoon lemon zest
    - 1 teaspoon lemon juice
    - 1 clove garlic, minced
    - Salt and black pepper to taste

Instructions:

1. **Prepare the Herb Butter:**
    - In a medium bowl, combine the softened butter with the parsley, chives, dill, lemon zest, lemon juice, and minced garlic. Mix well until all ingredients are evenly incorporated.
    - Season with salt and black pepper to taste.
    - Transfer the herb butter to a sheet of plastic wrap, shape it into a log, and refrigerate until firm (about 30 minutes). This step can be done in advance.
2. **Prepare the Sea Bass:**
    - Pat the sea bass fillets dry with paper towels to ensure a crispy sear.
    - Season both sides of the fillets with salt and black pepper.
3. **Pan-Seer the Sea Bass:**
    - Heat the olive oil in a large skillet over medium-high heat until shimmering.
    - Place the sea bass fillets in the skillet, skin-side down if applicable. Cook for 4-5 minutes without moving them, until the skin is crispy and the fillets are golden brown.
    - Carefully flip the fillets and cook for an additional 2-3 minutes, or until the fish is cooked through and flakes easily with a fork.
4. **Serve the Sea Bass:**
    - Transfer the cooked sea bass fillets to serving plates.
    - Slice the chilled herb butter into rounds and place a piece on top of each fillet. The heat from the fish will melt the butter and create a flavorful sauce.
    - Serve immediately, garnished with additional fresh herbs if desired.

Tips:

- **For a Crispy Skin:** Ensure the pan is hot before adding the fish and avoid moving it around until you're ready to flip it.
- **For Even Cooking:** Choose fillets of similar thickness for even cooking.
- **For a Flavor Boost:** Add a splash of white wine or a squeeze of fresh lemon juice to the pan after searing the fish for extra depth of flavor.

Enjoy your Pan-Seared Sea Bass with Herb Butter, a dish that's both luxurious and simple to make, perfect for any occasion!

Marionberry Smoothie

Ingredients:

- **For the Smoothie:**
    - 1 cup frozen marionberries (or frozen blackberries if marionberries are not available)
    - 1 banana, peeled and sliced
    - 1 cup plain or vanilla Greek yogurt
    - ½ cup milk (dairy or non-dairy like almond, oat, or soy milk)
    - 1-2 tablespoons honey or maple syrup (to taste)
    - 1 teaspoon vanilla extract (optional)
    - Ice cubes (optional, for a thicker smoothie)
- **For Garnish (Optional):**
    - Fresh marionberries or blackberries
    - Mint leaves
    - Granola

Instructions:

1. **Prepare the Ingredients:**
    - If using fresh marionberries, wash and freeze them beforehand. If you're using frozen marionberries, there's no need to thaw them.
2. **Blend the Smoothie:**
    - In a blender, combine the frozen marionberries, banana, Greek yogurt, milk, honey (or maple syrup), and vanilla extract (if using).
    - Blend on high until smooth and creamy. If the smoothie is too thick, you can add a little more milk to reach your desired consistency.
    - For a thicker smoothie, add a handful of ice cubes and blend again until smooth.
3. **Taste and Adjust:**
    - Taste the smoothie and adjust sweetness by adding more honey or maple syrup if needed.
4. **Serve:**
    - Pour the smoothie into glasses and garnish with fresh marionberries, mint leaves, or a sprinkle of granola if desired.

Tips:

- **For Added Nutrition:** You can add a handful of spinach or kale to the blender for a boost of greens without altering the flavor significantly.
- **For a Protein Boost:** Add a scoop of protein powder or a tablespoon of chia seeds or flaxseeds.
- **For a Creamier Texture:** Use full-fat Greek yogurt or a splash of coconut cream.

Enjoy your Marionberry Smoothie, a vibrant and tasty way to enjoy the delicious flavor of marionberries!

Creamy Mushroom Pasta

Ingredients:

- **For the Pasta:**
    - 12 ounces (340 grams) pasta (such as fettuccine, penne, or tagliatelle)
    - Salt, for seasoning the pasta water
- **For the Creamy Mushroom Sauce:**
    - 2 tablespoons unsalted butter
    - 1 tablespoon olive oil
    - 1 small onion, finely chopped
    - 3-4 garlic cloves, minced
    - 12 ounces (340 grams) mushrooms, sliced (cremini, button, or a mix)
    - ½ cup dry white wine (optional, or use vegetable broth)
    - 1 cup heavy cream
    - ½ cup grated Parmesan cheese
    - 1 teaspoon fresh thyme leaves (or ½ teaspoon dried thyme)
    - Salt and black pepper to taste
    - Fresh parsley, chopped (for garnish)

Instructions:

1. **Cook the Pasta:**
    - Bring a large pot of salted water to a boil. Cook the pasta according to the package instructions until al dente.
    - Reserve 1 cup of pasta water, then drain the pasta and set aside.
2. **Prepare the Creamy Mushroom Sauce:**
    - In a large skillet or sauté pan, heat the butter and olive oil over medium heat until the butter is melted.
    - Add the chopped onion and cook for 3-4 minutes until softened and translucent.
    - Add the minced garlic and cook for an additional 1 minute, until fragrant.
    - Add the sliced mushrooms and cook for 5-7 minutes, until they are golden brown and have released their moisture.
    - If using, pour in the white wine and let it simmer for 2-3 minutes, allowing it to reduce slightly. If not using wine, add vegetable broth at this stage.
    - Reduce the heat to low and stir in the heavy cream. Simmer gently for 2-3 minutes until the sauce thickens slightly.
3. **Finish the Sauce:**
    - Stir in the grated Parmesan cheese and fresh thyme. Season with salt and black pepper to taste.
    - If the sauce is too thick, add a small amount of the reserved pasta water to reach your desired consistency.
4. **Combine Pasta and Sauce:**

- Add the cooked pasta to the skillet with the creamy mushroom sauce. Toss gently to coat the pasta evenly with the sauce.
- Cook for an additional 1-2 minutes to allow the pasta to absorb some of the sauce.

5. **Serve:**
   - Divide the creamy mushroom pasta among serving plates.
   - Garnish with chopped fresh parsley and additional Parmesan cheese if desired.

Tips:

- **For Extra Flavor:** Add a splash of lemon juice or a pinch of nutmeg to the sauce for added depth.
- **For a Protein Boost:** You can add grilled chicken, sautéed shrimp, or crispy bacon to the pasta.
- **For a Vegetarian Option:** Ensure that the Parmesan cheese is vegetarian-friendly or use a plant-based alternative.

Enjoy your Creamy Mushroom Pasta, a luscious and satisfying dish that's perfect for any pasta lover!

Grilled Oysters with Garlic Butter

Ingredients:

- **For the Oysters:**
    - 12 large oysters, on the half shell (fresh and shucked)
    - Lemon wedges (for serving)
- **For the Garlic Butter:**
    - ½ cup unsalted butter, melted
    - 3-4 garlic cloves, minced
    - 2 tablespoons fresh parsley, finely chopped
    - 1 tablespoon fresh lemon juice
    - 1 teaspoon hot sauce (optional)
    - ¼ teaspoon salt
    - ¼ teaspoon black pepper

Instructions:

1. **Prepare the Garlic Butter:**
    - In a small bowl, combine the melted butter, minced garlic, chopped parsley, lemon juice, hot sauce (if using), salt, and black pepper. Mix well and set aside.
2. **Preheat the Grill:**
    - Preheat your grill to medium-high heat (about 400°F or 200°C). You can use a gas or charcoal grill for this recipe.
3. **Prepare the Oysters:**
    - Rinse the oysters under cold water to remove any sand or debris. Pat them dry with a paper towel.
    - Arrange the oysters on a grill-safe tray or directly on the grill grates if you prefer.
4. **Grill the Oysters:**
    - Place the oysters on the grill, shell-side down. Grill for 4-5 minutes, or until the oysters begin to open and are heated through. The oysters will start to bubble when they are ready.
5. **Add the Garlic Butter:**
    - Carefully spoon the garlic butter mixture over each oyster while they are still on the grill. Be generous with the butter for extra flavor.
    - Close the grill lid and cook for an additional 2-3 minutes to allow the garlic butter to melt and infuse the oysters.
6. **Serve:**
    - Remove the oysters from the grill and transfer them to a serving platter.
    - Serve immediately with lemon wedges on the side for squeezing over the oysters.

Tips:

- **For Extra Flavor:** You can add a sprinkle of grated Parmesan cheese or breadcrumbs on top of the garlic butter before grilling for a crispy topping.
- **For a Smoky Twist:** Add a few wood chips to the grill for a smoky flavor that complements the oysters.
- **For Safety:** Make sure the oysters are properly shucked and cleaned before grilling to avoid any potential contaminants.

Enjoy your Grilled Oysters with Garlic Butter, a simple yet indulgent seafood treat that's sure to impress your guests!

Oregon Cherry BBQ Sauce

Ingredients:

- **For the BBQ Sauce:**
    - 1 cup fresh or frozen Oregon cherries, pitted and halved (or use any sweet cherries)
    - 1 cup ketchup
    - ¼ cup apple cider vinegar
    - ¼ cup brown sugar
    - 2 tablespoons honey
    - 2 tablespoons Worcestershire sauce
    - 1 tablespoon soy sauce
    - 1 tablespoon Dijon mustard
    - 1 teaspoon smoked paprika
    - 1 teaspoon garlic powder
    - 1 teaspoon onion powder
    - ½ teaspoon ground black pepper
    - ¼ teaspoon salt
    - ¼ teaspoon red pepper flakes (optional, for heat)

Instructions:

1. **Prepare the Cherry Base:**
    - In a medium saucepan, combine the cherries with ½ cup of water.
    - Cook over medium heat, stirring occasionally, until the cherries are soft and have released their juices (about 10 minutes).
2. **Blend the Cherries:**
    - Use an immersion blender to puree the cherries in the saucepan until smooth. Alternatively, transfer the cherry mixture to a blender and blend until smooth, then return it to the saucepan.
3. **Combine the Ingredients:**
    - To the cherry puree, add the ketchup, apple cider vinegar, brown sugar, honey, Worcestershire sauce, soy sauce, Dijon mustard, smoked paprika, garlic powder, onion powder, black pepper, salt, and red pepper flakes (if using).
    - Stir well to combine all ingredients.
4. **Simmer the Sauce:**
    - Bring the mixture to a simmer over medium heat. Reduce the heat to low and let the sauce cook gently for 20-30 minutes, stirring occasionally, until it has thickened to your desired consistency.
5. **Adjust Seasoning:**
    - Taste the sauce and adjust seasoning as needed. You can add more salt, pepper, or honey to balance the flavors.
6. **Cool and Store:**

- Allow the sauce to cool to room temperature before using.
- Transfer to an airtight container and store in the refrigerator. The sauce can be kept for up to 2 weeks.

Tips:

- **For a Smokier Flavor:** Add a teaspoon of liquid smoke to the sauce during simmering.
- **For a Thicker Sauce:** Continue simmering the sauce for a longer time or add a cornstarch slurry (1 tablespoon cornstarch mixed with 1 tablespoon water) to thicken.
- **For Added Spice:** Increase the amount of red pepper flakes or add a dash of hot sauce.

Enjoy your Oregon Cherry BBQ Sauce with grilled meats, roasted vegetables, or as a flavorful dipping sauce!

Roasted Vegetable Medley

Ingredients:

- **For the Vegetables:**
    - 2 cups baby potatoes, halved
    - 1 large red bell pepper, cut into bite-sized pieces
    - 1 large yellow bell pepper, cut into bite-sized pieces
    - 1 large zucchini, sliced into half-moons
    - 1 cup carrots, sliced into rounds or sticks
    - 1 cup broccoli florets
    - 1 cup cherry tomatoes
    - 1 medium red onion, cut into wedges
    - 3-4 cloves garlic, minced
- **For the Seasoning:**
    - 3 tablespoons olive oil
    - 1 teaspoon dried thyme (or 2 teaspoons fresh thyme)
    - 1 teaspoon dried rosemary (or 2 teaspoons fresh rosemary)
    - 1 teaspoon dried oregano
    - 1 teaspoon paprika
    - Salt and black pepper to taste
    - 1 tablespoon balsamic vinegar (optional, for added flavor)

Instructions:

1. **Preheat the Oven:**
    - Preheat your oven to 425°F (220°C). Line a large baking sheet with parchment paper or lightly grease it.
2. **Prepare the Vegetables:**
    - Wash and cut the vegetables into uniform sizes to ensure even roasting. For example, halve the potatoes and cut the bell peppers into similar-sized pieces.
3. **Season the Vegetables:**
    - In a large bowl, combine the olive oil, dried thyme, dried rosemary, dried oregano, paprika, salt, and black pepper. Stir well to combine.
    - Add the prepared vegetables and minced garlic to the bowl. Toss until all the vegetables are evenly coated with the seasoning mixture.
4. **Roast the Vegetables:**
    - Spread the seasoned vegetables out in a single layer on the prepared baking sheet. Make sure they are not overcrowded to ensure they roast properly and become crispy.
    - Roast in the preheated oven for 25-35 minutes, or until the vegetables are tender and nicely caramelized. Toss the vegetables halfway through the cooking time for even roasting.
5. **Finish and Serve:**

- If desired, drizzle the roasted vegetables with balsamic vinegar right before serving for extra flavor.
- Garnish with fresh herbs like parsley or basil if you like.

Tips:

- **For Even Roasting:** Cut vegetables into similar sizes and avoid overcrowding the baking sheet. Use two baking sheets if necessary.
- **For Extra Flavor:** Add a sprinkle of Parmesan cheese or a squeeze of lemon juice after roasting.
- **For a Mediterranean Twist:** Use vegetables like eggplant, squash, and olives, and add a sprinkle of feta cheese.

Enjoy your Roasted Vegetable Medley as a delicious and nutritious side dish or a flavorful main course!

Hazelnut-Coffee Brownies

Ingredients:

- **For the Brownies:**
    - 1 cup (2 sticks) unsalted butter
    - 1 cup granulated sugar
    - 2 large eggs
    - 1 teaspoon vanilla extract
    - 1/2 cup unsweetened cocoa powder
    - 1/2 cup all-purpose flour
    - 1/4 teaspoon salt
    - 1/4 teaspoon baking powder
    - 1/2 cup finely chopped hazelnuts
    - 1 tablespoon instant coffee granules or espresso powder
- **For the Ganache (Optional):**
    - 1/2 cup heavy cream
    - 1/2 cup semisweet chocolate chips
    - 1 tablespoon unsalted butter

Instructions:

1. **Preheat the Oven:**
    - Preheat your oven to 350°F (175°C). Grease and flour an 8x8-inch baking pan, or line it with parchment paper for easy removal.
2. **Prepare the Brownie Batter:**
    - In a medium saucepan, melt the butter over low heat. Remove from heat and stir in the granulated sugar until combined.
    - Add the eggs one at a time, beating well after each addition. Stir in the vanilla extract.
    - In a separate bowl, whisk together the cocoa powder, flour, salt, and baking powder.
    - Gradually add the dry ingredients to the butter mixture, stirring until just combined.
    - Dissolve the instant coffee granules or espresso powder in a small amount of hot water (about 1 tablespoon) and mix into the batter.
    - Fold in the chopped hazelnuts.
3. **Bake the Brownies:**
    - Pour the batter into the prepared baking pan and spread it evenly.
    - Bake in the preheated oven for 25-30 minutes, or until a toothpick inserted into the center comes out with a few moist crumbs.
    - Let the brownies cool in the pan on a wire rack before cutting into squares.
4. **Prepare the Ganache (Optional):**

- While the brownies are cooling, heat the heavy cream in a small saucepan over medium heat until it just begins to simmer.
              - Remove from heat and add the chocolate chips, stirring until the chocolate is completely melted and smooth.
              - Stir in the butter until fully combined and glossy.
              - Once the brownies are completely cool, spread the ganache over the top or drizzle it for a decorative touch.
5. **Serve:**
              - Cut the brownies into squares and serve.

Tips:

- **For Extra Texture:** Toast the hazelnuts before chopping to enhance their flavor.
- **For a Coffee Boost:** Increase the amount of instant coffee or espresso powder for a stronger coffee flavor.
- **For a Fun Twist:** Add a sprinkle of sea salt on top of the ganache before it sets for a sweet and salty contrast.

Enjoy your Hazelnut-Coffee Brownies, a delicious blend of rich chocolate, nutty hazelnuts, and aromatic coffee!

Smoked Salmon Bagels

Ingredients:

- **For the Bagels:**
  - 4 plain or sesame bagels, split and toasted
- **For the Cream Cheese Spread:**
  - 8 ounces (225 grams) cream cheese, softened
  - 2 tablespoons fresh dill, finely chopped (or 1 tablespoon dried dill)
  - 1 tablespoon fresh chives, finely chopped
  - 1 tablespoon lemon juice
  - 1 teaspoon Dijon mustard (optional)
  - Salt and black pepper to taste
- **For the Toppings:**
  - 4 ounces (115 grams) smoked salmon, sliced
  - 1 small red onion, thinly sliced
  - 1-2 tablespoons capers, drained
  - 1 tomato, thinly sliced
  - Fresh dill sprigs (for garnish)
  - Lemon wedges (for serving)

Instructions:

1. **Prepare the Cream Cheese Spread:**
   - In a medium bowl, combine the softened cream cheese, fresh dill, chives, lemon juice, and Dijon mustard (if using).
   - Mix until smooth and well combined. Season with salt and black pepper to taste.
   - Set aside.
2. **Toast the Bagels:**
   - Split the bagels and toast them until golden brown. You can use a toaster or toast them under a broiler.
3. **Assemble the Bagels:**
   - Spread a generous layer of the cream cheese mixture on each toasted bagel half.
   - Top with slices of smoked salmon.
4. **Add the Toppings:**
   - Arrange slices of red onion, capers, and tomato over the smoked salmon.
   - Garnish with additional fresh dill sprigs.
5. **Serve:**
   - Serve the smoked salmon bagels immediately, with lemon wedges on the side for squeezing over the top.

Tips:

- **For a Creamier Spread:** Mix in a tablespoon of sour cream or Greek yogurt with the cream cheese.
- **For Extra Flavor:** Add a dash of hot sauce or a sprinkle of everything bagel seasoning to the cream cheese spread.
- **For a Variation:** Add thin slices of cucumber or avocado for added freshness and flavor.

Enjoy your Smoked Salmon Bagels, a delightful combination of creamy, savory, and fresh ingredients that's sure to please!

Pear and Gorgonzola Salad

Ingredients:

- **For the Salad:**
    - 6 cups mixed salad greens (e.g., arugula, baby spinach, and baby greens)
    - 2 ripe pears, cored and sliced thinly
    - 1/2 cup crumbled Gorgonzola cheese
    - 1/4 cup toasted walnuts or pecans
    - 1/4 cup dried cranberries or cherries (optional)
    - 1/4 red onion, thinly sliced (optional)
- **For the Dressing:**
    - 1/4 cup extra virgin olive oil
    - 2 tablespoons balsamic vinegar
    - 1 tablespoon honey
    - 1 teaspoon Dijon mustard
    - Salt and black pepper to taste

Instructions:

1. **Prepare the Dressing:**
    - In a small bowl or jar, combine the olive oil, balsamic vinegar, honey, and Dijon mustard.
    - Whisk or shake until well combined and emulsified.
    - Season with salt and black pepper to taste. Adjust the seasoning as needed.
2. **Assemble the Salad:**
    - In a large salad bowl, place the mixed greens.
    - Top with sliced pears, crumbled Gorgonzola cheese, and toasted walnuts or pecans.
    - If using, add dried cranberries or cherries and thinly sliced red onion.
3. **Dress the Salad:**
    - Just before serving, drizzle the dressing over the salad.
    - Gently toss to coat the ingredients evenly with the dressing.
4. **Serve:**
    - Serve immediately to enjoy the fresh and crisp flavors.

Tips:

- **For Extra Flavor:** Add a sprinkle of fresh herbs such as mint or thyme.
- **For Crunch:** Consider adding thinly sliced apples or cucumber for additional texture.
- **For a Hearty Meal:** Incorporate grilled chicken or sliced steak as a topping.

Enjoy your Pear and Gorgonzola Salad, a harmonious mix of sweet, tangy, and savory flavors that's both sophisticated and satisfying!

Oregon Chardonnay Chicken

Ingredients:

- **For the Chicken:**
    - 4 boneless, skinless chicken breasts
    - Salt and black pepper to taste
    - 2 tablespoons olive oil
    - 2 tablespoons all-purpose flour (for dredging)
- **For the Chardonnay Sauce:**
    - 1 cup Oregon Chardonnay (or other dry white wine)
    - 1/2 cup chicken broth
    - 1 small onion, finely chopped
    - 3 cloves garlic, minced
    - 1 tablespoon fresh thyme leaves (or 1 teaspoon dried thyme)
    - 1 tablespoon fresh parsley, chopped (for garnish)
    - 2 tablespoons unsalted butter
    - 1 tablespoon Dijon mustard
    - 1 tablespoon lemon juice
    - Salt and black pepper to taste

Instructions:

1. **Prepare the Chicken:**
    - Season the chicken breasts with salt and black pepper.
    - Dredge each chicken breast in flour, shaking off the excess.
2. **Cook the Chicken:**
    - In a large skillet, heat the olive oil over medium-high heat.
    - Add the chicken breasts and cook for 5-7 minutes per side, or until golden brown and cooked through (internal temperature should reach 165°F or 74°C).
    - Remove the chicken from the skillet and set aside. Cover with foil to keep warm.
3. **Make the Chardonnay Sauce:**
    - In the same skillet, add the chopped onion and cook for 3-4 minutes until softened.
    - Add the minced garlic and cook for an additional 1 minute, until fragrant.
    - Pour in the Chardonnay and chicken broth, stirring to combine and deglaze the pan.
    - Stir in the fresh thyme and bring the mixture to a simmer. Let it cook for 5-7 minutes, or until the sauce has reduced slightly.
4. **Finish the Sauce:**
    - Reduce the heat to low and whisk in the butter until melted and the sauce is smooth.
    - Stir in the Dijon mustard and lemon juice. Season with salt and black pepper to taste.

- Return the chicken breasts to the skillet and spoon some of the sauce over them. Let them simmer in the sauce for a few minutes to reheat and absorb the flavors.
5. **Serve:**
    - Transfer the chicken breasts to serving plates and spoon the Chardonnay sauce over the top.
    - Garnish with chopped fresh parsley.

Tips:

- **For a Richer Sauce:** You can add a splash of cream or a bit of grated Parmesan cheese to the sauce for extra richness.
- **For More Vegetables:** Include sautéed mushrooms, spinach, or artichoke hearts in the sauce.
- **For a Side Dish:** Serve the chicken with mashed potatoes, rice, or steamed vegetables to complete the meal.

Enjoy your Oregon Chardonnay Chicken, a delectable dish with the perfect balance of savory and wine-infused flavors!

Blackberry-Walnut Bread

Ingredients:

- **For the Bread:**
    - 1 ½ cups all-purpose flour
    - 1 teaspoon baking powder
    - ½ teaspoon baking soda
    - ¼ teaspoon salt
    - ½ cup granulated sugar
    - 1/3 cup brown sugar, packed
    - 1/3 cup vegetable oil or melted butter
    - 1 large egg
    - 1 teaspoon vanilla extract
    - 1 cup fresh or frozen blackberries (if using frozen, do not thaw)
    - ½ cup chopped walnuts
- **For Optional Glaze (if desired):**
    - 1/4 cup powdered sugar
    - 1 tablespoon milk or lemon juice

Instructions:

1. **Preheat the Oven:**
    - Preheat your oven to 350°F (175°C).
    - Grease and flour a 9x5-inch loaf pan, or line it with parchment paper for easy removal.
2. **Prepare the Dry Ingredients:**
    - In a medium bowl, whisk together the flour, baking powder, baking soda, and salt. Set aside.
3. **Mix the Wet Ingredients:**
    - In a large bowl, combine the granulated sugar, brown sugar, and vegetable oil (or melted butter).
    - Add the egg and vanilla extract, and beat until well combined.
4. **Combine the Ingredients:**
    - Gradually add the dry ingredients to the wet ingredients, stirring until just combined.
    - Gently fold in the blackberries and chopped walnuts. Be careful not to overmix, as this can make the bread dense.
5. **Bake the Bread:**
    - Pour the batter into the prepared loaf pan and spread it evenly.
    - Bake in the preheated oven for 50-60 minutes, or until a toothpick inserted into the center of the loaf comes out clean or with just a few moist crumbs.
6. **Cool and Glaze (Optional):**

- Let the bread cool in the pan for about 10 minutes, then transfer it to a wire rack to cool completely.
- If using the glaze, whisk together the powdered sugar and milk (or lemon juice) until smooth. Drizzle over the cooled bread.

7. **Serve:**
   - Slice and serve the Blackberry-Walnut Bread at room temperature.

Tips:

- **For Even Distribution:** Toss the blackberries in a bit of flour before folding them into the batter to help prevent them from sinking to the bottom.
- **For Extra Flavor:** Add a teaspoon of cinnamon or nutmeg to the dry ingredients for a warm, spiced flavor.
- **For a Crunchy Top:** Sprinkle a few extra chopped walnuts on top of the batter before baking.

Enjoy your Blackberry-Walnut Bread, a deliciously moist and flavorful treat with a delightful combination of sweet berries and crunchy walnuts!

Crab and Corn Chowder

Ingredients:

- **For the Chowder:**
    - 4 tablespoons unsalted butter
    - 1 medium onion, finely chopped
    - 2 cloves garlic, minced
    - 2 celery stalks, diced
    - 2 medium carrots, diced
    - 1 cup diced potatoes (about 2 small potatoes)
    - 3 cups fresh or frozen corn kernels (about 4 ears of corn if fresh)
    - 3 cups chicken broth
    - 1 cup heavy cream
    - 1 cup whole milk
    - 12 ounces lump crab meat, picked over for shells
    - 1 teaspoon Old Bay seasoning
    - 1/2 teaspoon dried thyme
    - Salt and black pepper to taste
    - 2 tablespoons fresh parsley, chopped (for garnish)
    - Lemon wedges (for serving)

Instructions:

1. **Prepare the Vegetables:**
    - In a large pot or Dutch oven, melt the butter over medium heat.
    - Add the chopped onion, garlic, celery, and carrots. Cook for about 5-7 minutes, until the vegetables are softened and the onion is translucent.
2. **Cook the Potatoes:**
    - Add the diced potatoes to the pot and cook for an additional 5 minutes, stirring occasionally.
3. **Add Corn and Broth:**
    - Stir in the corn kernels, chicken broth, Old Bay seasoning, and dried thyme.
    - Bring the mixture to a boil, then reduce the heat and let it simmer for about 10-15 minutes, or until the potatoes are tender.
4. **Add Cream and Milk:**
    - Stir in the heavy cream and milk. Continue to cook over low heat until the chowder is heated through.
5. **Incorporate the Crab Meat:**
    - Gently fold in the lump crab meat and cook for an additional 3-5 minutes, just until the crab is heated through. Be careful not to stir too vigorously to avoid breaking up the crab meat.
6. **Season and Garnish:**
    - Taste the chowder and adjust the seasoning with salt and black pepper if needed.

- Garnish with chopped fresh parsley.
7. **Serve:**
   - Ladle the chowder into bowls and serve with lemon wedges on the side.

Tips:

- **For Extra Flavor:** Consider adding a splash of sherry or white wine to the chowder for depth.
- **For a Thicker Chowder:** You can mash some of the potatoes with a fork or use an immersion blender to puree part of the chowder, then stir it back in.
- **For Fresh Corn:** If using fresh corn, cut the kernels off the cob and add them directly to the pot. You can also scrape the cobs to release additional corn milk into the chowder for extra flavor.

Enjoy your Crab and Corn Chowder, a rich and satisfying soup perfect for any occasion!

Huckleberry Crumble Bars

Ingredients:

- **For the Crust and Crumble Topping:**
    - 1 ¾ cups all-purpose flour
    - ½ cup granulated sugar
    - ½ teaspoon baking powder
    - ¼ teaspoon salt
    - ½ cup unsalted butter, cold and cut into small pieces
    - 1 large egg yolk
- **For the Huckleberry Filling:**
    - 2 cups fresh or frozen huckleberries (if using frozen, do not thaw)
    - ½ cup granulated sugar
    - 1 tablespoon cornstarch
    - 1 tablespoon lemon juice
    - ¼ teaspoon ground cinnamon (optional)

Instructions:

1. **Preheat the Oven:**
    - Preheat your oven to 350°F (175°C).
    - Line an 8x8-inch baking pan with parchment paper, leaving a slight overhang for easy removal.
2. **Prepare the Crust and Crumble Topping:**
    - In a large bowl, whisk together the flour, sugar, baking powder, and salt.
    - Add the cold butter pieces to the flour mixture. Use a pastry cutter or your fingers to work the butter into the flour until the mixture resembles coarse crumbs.
    - Stir in the egg yolk until the mixture starts to come together. The dough will be somewhat crumbly but should hold together when pressed.
3. **Press the Dough:**
    - Reserve 1 cup of the crumble mixture for the topping.
    - Press the remaining mixture evenly into the bottom of the prepared baking pan to form the crust.
4. **Prepare the Huckleberry Filling:**
    - In a medium saucepan, combine the huckleberries, sugar, cornstarch, lemon juice, and cinnamon (if using).
    - Cook over medium heat, stirring occasionally, until the mixture comes to a boil and thickens. This should take about 5-7 minutes.
    - Remove from heat and let the filling cool slightly.
5. **Assemble the Bars:**
    - Pour the huckleberry filling over the prepared crust, spreading it evenly.
    - Sprinkle the reserved crumble mixture evenly over the huckleberry filling.
6. **Bake the Bars:**
    - Bake in the preheated oven for 30-35 minutes, or until the topping is golden brown and the filling is bubbly.

7. **Cool and Slice:**
   - Allow the bars to cool completely in the pan on a wire rack.
   - Once cooled, lift the bars out of the pan using the parchment paper overhang and cut into squares.

Tips:

- **For Even Crumbles:** Make sure to evenly distribute the crumble topping for a consistent texture.
- **For a Flavor Twist:** Add a pinch of nutmeg to the huckleberry filling for extra depth of flavor.
- **For a Sweeter Filling:** Adjust the sugar in the filling to your taste, especially if your huckleberries are very tart.

Enjoy your Huckleberry Crumble Bars as a delightful dessert or snack with a cup of tea or coffee!

BBQ Chicken with Oregon Fruit Glaze

Ingredients:

- **For the BBQ Chicken:**
    - 4 bone-in, skinless chicken thighs (or your preferred chicken parts)
    - Salt and black pepper to taste
    - 1 tablespoon olive oil
- **For the Oregon Fruit Glaze:**
    - 1 cup Oregon fruit juice (such as raspberry, blackberry, or cherry, or a blend of these)
    - 1/2 cup granulated sugar
    - 1 tablespoon cornstarch
    - 2 tablespoons water
    - 1 tablespoon balsamic vinegar
    - 1 tablespoon soy sauce
    - 1 teaspoon fresh ginger, grated (optional)
    - 1 garlic clove, minced (optional)
- **For Garnish:**
    - Fresh herbs (like parsley or cilantro), chopped
    - Lemon or lime wedges (optional)

Instructions:

1. **Prepare the Glaze:**
    - In a small saucepan, combine the fruit juice and granulated sugar.
    - In a separate small bowl, mix the cornstarch with the water to make a slurry.
    - Add the cornstarch slurry to the saucepan, stirring constantly.
    - Bring the mixture to a simmer over medium heat, stirring until the glaze thickens, about 5-7 minutes.
    - Stir in the balsamic vinegar, soy sauce, and optional ginger and garlic. Cook for another minute or two.
    - Remove from heat and set aside.
2. **Prepare the Chicken:**
    - Preheat your grill to medium-high heat.
    - Season the chicken thighs with salt and black pepper.
    - Brush the grill grates with olive oil to prevent sticking.
3. **Grill the Chicken:**
    - Place the chicken thighs on the grill and cook for about 6-8 minutes per side, or until the internal temperature reaches 165°F (74°C) and the chicken is nicely charred.
    - During the last few minutes of grilling, brush the chicken with the Oregon fruit glaze, turning occasionally to ensure even coating.
4. **Serve:**
    - Remove the chicken from the grill and let it rest for a few minutes.
    - Brush the chicken with additional glaze if desired.

- Garnish with chopped fresh herbs and serve with lemon or lime wedges if desired.

Tips:

- **For a Smoky Flavor:** Add a few wood chips to the grill for extra smoky flavor.
- **For Extra Crispiness:** Allow the chicken to cook without moving it too frequently to get a nice char.
- **For a Fruity Twist:** Experiment with different Oregon fruit juices or combinations to find your favorite glaze flavor.

Enjoy your BBQ Chicken with Oregon Fruit Glaze, a deliciously unique dish that brings together smoky, sweet, and tangy flavors!

Grilled Portobello Mushrooms

Ingredients:

- **For the Marinade:**
    - 1/4 cup extra virgin olive oil
    - 2 tablespoons balsamic vinegar
    - 2 tablespoons soy sauce
    - 2 cloves garlic, minced
    - 1 tablespoon fresh rosemary or thyme, chopped (or 1 teaspoon dried)
    - 1 teaspoon Dijon mustard
    - 1 teaspoon honey (optional)
    - Salt and black pepper to taste
- **For the Mushrooms:**
    - 4 large Portobello mushrooms, stems removed and gills scraped out
    - Fresh herbs for garnish (optional)
    - Lemon wedges for serving (optional)

Instructions:

1. **Prepare the Marinade:**
    - In a small bowl, whisk together the olive oil, balsamic vinegar, soy sauce, minced garlic, chopped rosemary or thyme, Dijon mustard, honey (if using), salt, and black pepper.
2. **Marinate the Mushrooms:**
    - Place the Portobello mushrooms in a large resealable plastic bag or shallow dish.
    - Pour the marinade over the mushrooms, making sure they are well coated.
    - Seal the bag or cover the dish and marinate in the refrigerator for at least 30 minutes, or up to 2 hours for more flavor.
3. **Preheat the Grill:**
    - Preheat your grill to medium-high heat (about 375-450°F or 190-230°C).
4. **Grill the Mushrooms:**
    - Remove the mushrooms from the marinade and discard the marinade.
    - Place the mushrooms on the grill, gill side down. Grill for about 4-5 minutes per side, or until they are tender and have nice grill marks. Avoid pressing down on the mushrooms to keep them juicy.
5. **Serve:**
    - Transfer the grilled mushrooms to a serving platter.
    - Garnish with fresh herbs if desired.
    - Serve with lemon wedges on the side for an extra burst of freshness.

Tips:

- **For Extra Flavor:** Add a sprinkle of grated Parmesan cheese or a drizzle of balsamic reduction after grilling.

- **For a Smokier Taste:** Use a wood-chip smoker box or add soaked wood chips to the grill.
- **For a Heartier Dish:** Serve the grilled Portobello mushrooms on a bun as a burger alternative or sliced over a salad.

Enjoy your Grilled Portobello Mushrooms, a savory and satisfying dish that's perfect for any occasion!

Marionberry and Almond Tart

Ingredients:

- **For the Tart Crust:**
    - 1 ¼ cups all-purpose flour
    - ¼ cup granulated sugar
    - ½ teaspoon salt
    - ½ cup unsalted butter, cold and cut into small pieces
    - 1 large egg yolk
    - 2 tablespoons ice water (more if needed)
- **For the Almond Filling:**
    - ½ cup unsalted butter, softened
    - ½ cup granulated sugar
    - ½ cup almond meal (or finely ground almonds)
    - 2 large eggs
    - 1 teaspoon vanilla extract
    - ¼ teaspoon almond extract
    - ¼ cup all-purpose flour
- **For the Marionberry Filling:**
    - 2 cups fresh or frozen Marionberries (if using frozen, do not thaw)
    - ¼ cup granulated sugar
    - 2 tablespoons cornstarch
    - 1 tablespoon lemon juice
- **For Garnish (optional):**
    - Powdered sugar for dusting
    - Fresh mint leaves

Instructions:

1. **Prepare the Tart Crust:**
    - In a medium bowl, whisk together the flour, sugar, and salt.
    - Add the cold butter pieces and use a pastry cutter or your fingers to work the butter into the flour mixture until it resembles coarse crumbs.
    - Stir in the egg yolk and ice water until the dough comes together. You may need to add a bit more ice water if the dough is too dry.
    - Shape the dough into a disc, wrap it in plastic wrap, and refrigerate for at least 30 minutes.
2. **Preheat the Oven:**
    - Preheat your oven to 350°F (175°C).
3. **Roll Out the Dough:**
    - On a lightly floured surface, roll out the dough to fit a 9-inch tart pan with a removable bottom.
    - Carefully transfer the dough to the tart pan, pressing it into the bottom and up the sides. Trim any excess dough.
    - Chill the tart shell in the refrigerator for 15 minutes.

4. **Pre-Bake the Crust:**
    - Line the tart shell with parchment paper and fill it with pie weights or dried beans.
    - Bake in the preheated oven for 15 minutes.
    - Remove the parchment paper and weights, and bake for an additional 5 minutes until the crust is lightly golden. Let it cool slightly.
5. **Prepare the Almond Filling:**
    - In a large bowl, beat the softened butter and sugar until creamy.
    - Add the almond meal, eggs, vanilla extract, and almond extract, and mix until well combined.
    - Stir in the flour until the mixture is smooth.
6. **Prepare the Marionberry Filling:**
    - In a medium saucepan, combine the Marionberries, sugar, cornstarch, and lemon juice.
    - Cook over medium heat, stirring occasionally, until the mixture thickens and the berries release their juices, about 5-7 minutes.
    - Remove from heat and let it cool slightly.
7. **Assemble the Tart:**
    - Spread the almond filling evenly over the pre-baked tart crust.
    - Spoon the Marionberry filling over the almond filling, spreading it evenly.
8. **Bake the Tart:**
    - Bake in the preheated oven for 30-35 minutes, or until the almond filling is set and the top is golden brown.
    - Allow the tart to cool completely before removing from the pan.
9. **Serve:**
    - Dust the tart with powdered sugar if desired and garnish with fresh mint leaves.

Tips:

- **For a More Intense Flavor:** Consider adding a teaspoon of lemon zest to the Marionberry filling.
- **For a Crunchier Crust:** Bake the crust a little longer during the pre-baking phase.
- **For a Beautiful Finish:** Brush the Marionberry filling with a bit of warmed apricot jam for a glossy finish.

Enjoy your Marionberry and Almond Tart, a delightful blend of fruity and nutty flavors in a perfect, crisp tart shell!

Wild Mushroom and Goat Cheese Pizza

Ingredients:

- **For the Pizza Dough:**
    - 2 ¼ teaspoons active dry yeast (1 packet)
    - 1 ½ cups warm water (110°F or 45°C)
    - 3 ½ to 4 cups all-purpose flour
    - 2 tablespoons olive oil
    - 1 teaspoon sugar
    - 1 teaspoon salt
- **For the Pizza Topping:**
    - 1 tablespoon olive oil
    - 2 cups mixed wild mushrooms, sliced (such as shiitake, oyster, and cremini)
    - 2 cloves garlic, minced
    - 1 teaspoon fresh thyme leaves (or ½ teaspoon dried thyme)
    - Salt and black pepper to taste
    - 1 cup shredded mozzarella cheese
    - 4 ounces goat cheese, crumbled
    - ¼ cup grated Parmesan cheese
    - 1 tablespoon fresh parsley, chopped (for garnish)
    - 1 tablespoon balsamic glaze (optional, for drizzling)

Instructions:

1. **Prepare the Pizza Dough:**
    - In a small bowl, dissolve the yeast and sugar in the warm water. Let it sit for about 5-10 minutes, or until frothy.
    - In a large bowl, combine 3 ½ cups of flour and salt.
    - Make a well in the center and add the yeast mixture and olive oil.
    - Stir until the dough begins to come together. Add more flour if needed, a little at a time, until the dough is smooth and elastic.
    - Turn the dough out onto a floured surface and knead for about 5-7 minutes.
    - Place the dough in a lightly oiled bowl, cover it with a damp cloth, and let it rise in a warm place for about 1 hour, or until doubled in size.
2. **Prepare the Mushrooms:**
    - While the dough is rising, heat 1 tablespoon of olive oil in a skillet over medium heat.
    - Add the sliced mushrooms and cook for about 5-7 minutes, or until they are tender and have released their moisture.
    - Stir in the minced garlic and thyme. Season with salt and black pepper.
    - Cook for an additional 1-2 minutes, then remove from heat and set aside.
3. **Preheat the Oven:**
    - Preheat your oven to 475°F (245°C). If using a pizza stone, place it in the oven to preheat as well.
4. **Assemble the Pizza:**

- Punch down the risen dough and divide it into 2 equal portions (for two 12-inch pizzas) or keep it whole for one large pizza.
- Roll out the dough on a floured surface to your desired thickness.
- Transfer the rolled-out dough to a lightly floured pizza peel or baking sheet.
- Spread a thin layer of shredded mozzarella cheese over the dough.
- Evenly distribute the cooked mushrooms over the cheese.
- Crumble the goat cheese over the mushrooms.
- Sprinkle with grated Parmesan cheese.

5. **Bake the Pizza:**
    - Bake in the preheated oven for 12-15 minutes, or until the crust is golden brown and the cheese is melted and bubbly.
    - If using a pizza stone, transfer the pizza to the stone and bake as directed.
6. **Finish and Serve:**
    - Remove the pizza from the oven and let it cool slightly.
    - Garnish with chopped fresh parsley and drizzle with balsamic glaze if desired.
    - Slice and serve hot.

Tips:

- **For a Crispier Crust:** Preheat your pizza stone in the oven for at least 30 minutes before baking.
- **For Extra Flavor:** Add a pinch of red pepper flakes or a drizzle of truffle oil for an extra touch.
- **For a More Gourmet Touch:** Experiment with additional toppings like caramelized onions or fresh arugula.

Enjoy your Wild Mushroom and Goat Cheese Pizza, a delightful combination of earthy mushrooms and creamy cheese on a perfect, crisp crust!

Oregon Cherry-Lime Sorbet

Ingredients:

- **For the Cherry-Lime Sorbet:**
  - 4 cups fresh or frozen Oregon cherries (pitted)
  - 1 cup granulated sugar
  - 1 cup water
  - ½ cup freshly squeezed lime juice (about 3-4 limes)
  - 1 tablespoon lime zest
  - 1 teaspoon vanilla extract (optional)
  - Pinch of salt

Instructions:

1. **Prepare the Cherry Puree:**
   - If using fresh cherries, pit them and cut them in half. If using frozen cherries, let them thaw slightly.
   - In a blender or food processor, blend the cherries until smooth. You should have about 3 cups of cherry puree.
2. **Make the Syrup:**
   - In a medium saucepan, combine the water and granulated sugar.
   - Heat over medium heat, stirring constantly, until the sugar is fully dissolved. This should take about 2-3 minutes.
   - Remove from heat and let the syrup cool to room temperature.
3. **Combine Ingredients:**
   - In a large bowl, combine the cherry puree, cooled syrup, freshly squeezed lime juice, lime zest, and vanilla extract (if using).
   - Stir until everything is well mixed.
4. **Chill the Mixture:**
   - Cover the mixture and refrigerate for at least 1-2 hours, or until it is thoroughly chilled.
5. **Process in an Ice Cream Maker:**
   - Pour the chilled mixture into an ice cream maker and churn according to the manufacturer's instructions. This usually takes about 20-25 minutes.
   - The sorbet should be soft and creamy once churned.
6. **Freeze:**
   - Transfer the churned sorbet to an airtight container and freeze for at least 2 hours, or until firm.
7. **Serve:**
   - Scoop the sorbet into bowls or cones and enjoy!

Tips:

- **For a Smoother Texture:** If you prefer an even smoother sorbet, you can strain the cherry puree through a fine-mesh sieve before mixing with the syrup.
- **For a Flavor Twist:** Add a few fresh mint leaves to the cherry mixture before chilling for a hint of mint flavor.

- **For a Balanced Sweetness:** Taste the mixture before churning and adjust the sweetness if necessary by adding more sugar or lime juice.

Enjoy your Oregon Cherry-Lime Sorbet, a delightful and refreshing dessert that's perfect for warm weather and cherry season!

Pan-Roasted Duck Breast

Ingredients:

- **For the Duck Breast:**
    - 4 duck breasts (about 6-8 ounces each)
    - Salt and black pepper to taste
    - 1 teaspoon dried thyme (optional)
    - 1 tablespoon olive oil (if needed)
- **For the Glaze (optional but recommended):**
    - 1/2 cup red wine (such as Pinot Noir or Merlot)
    - 1/4 cup balsamic vinegar
    - 2 tablespoons honey or maple syrup
    - 1 teaspoon Dijon mustard
    - 1 tablespoon finely chopped fresh rosemary or thyme

Instructions:

1. **Prepare the Duck Breasts:**
    - Pat the duck breasts dry with paper towels.
    - Score the skin of each duck breast in a crosshatch pattern, being careful not to cut into the meat.
    - Season both sides of the duck breasts generously with salt, black pepper, and dried thyme (if using).
2. **Sear the Duck Breasts:**
    - Heat a large, oven-safe skillet over medium-high heat. You should not need additional oil if the duck breasts have enough fat.
    - Once the skillet is hot, place the duck breasts skin-side down in the pan. You should hear a sizzling sound.
    - Cook the duck breasts without moving them for about 6-8 minutes, or until the skin is crispy and golden brown. The fat should render out during this time.
    - Flip the duck breasts over and cook for an additional 2-3 minutes for medium-rare, or longer if desired. For medium, aim for 4-5 minutes on the meat side.
    - Transfer the skillet to the preheated oven if you prefer to cook them further or to keep them warm. Bake at 375°F (190°C) for 4-6 minutes for medium-rare.
3. **Rest the Duck Breasts:**
    - Remove the duck breasts from the skillet and let them rest on a cutting board for about 5 minutes before slicing. This allows the juices to redistribute.
4. **Prepare the Glaze (Optional):**
    - While the duck is resting, make the glaze. In the same skillet used for the duck, discard any excess fat, leaving about 1 tablespoon in the pan.
    - Add the red wine to the skillet and bring it to a simmer over medium heat, scraping up any browned bits from the bottom of the pan.
    - Stir in the balsamic vinegar, honey or maple syrup, Dijon mustard, and chopped rosemary or thyme.
    - Simmer the glaze for about 5-7 minutes, or until it has reduced and thickened to your desired consistency.

- Season with salt and pepper to taste.
5. **Serve:**
   - Slice the duck breasts against the grain and arrange them on a serving plate.
   - Drizzle with the prepared glaze or serve it on the side.
   - Garnish with additional fresh herbs if desired.

Tips:

- **For Perfect Crispy Skin:** Make sure the duck breasts are thoroughly dried before searing and avoid moving them around too much in the pan.
- **For a Richer Glaze:** Add a tablespoon of duck or chicken stock to the glaze for extra depth of flavor.
- **For a Balanced Meal:** Serve with roasted vegetables or a light salad to complement the richness of the duck.

Enjoy your Pan-Roasted Duck Breast, a delectable and elegant dish that's sure to impress!

Oregon White Wine Mussels

Ingredients:

- **For the Mussels:**
    - 2 pounds fresh mussels, scrubbed and debearded
    - 1 tablespoon olive oil
    - 4 cloves garlic, minced
    - 1 small onion, finely chopped
    - 1 cup Oregon white wine (such as Pinot Gris or Chardonnay)
    - 1 cup chicken or vegetable broth
    - 1/4 cup fresh parsley, chopped
    - 1 tablespoon fresh thyme leaves (or 1 teaspoon dried thyme)
    - 1 teaspoon lemon zest (optional)
    - Salt and black pepper to taste
    - Lemon wedges for serving (optional)
- **For Garnish (optional):**
    - Fresh parsley, chopped
    - Crusty bread for dipping

Instructions:

1. **Prepare the Mussels:**
    - Rinse the mussels under cold water. Scrub the shells with a brush to remove any dirt. Remove any beards by pulling them off with your fingers or a knife.
    - Discard any mussels with cracked shells or those that do not close when tapped.
2. **Cook the Aromatics:**
    - In a large pot or Dutch oven, heat the olive oil over medium heat.
    - Add the minced garlic and finely chopped onion. Sauté for about 2-3 minutes, or until the onion is translucent and the garlic is fragrant.
3. **Add the Liquids:**
    - Pour in the Oregon white wine and chicken or vegetable broth. Bring the mixture to a simmer.
    - Add the fresh thyme, lemon zest (if using), and season with salt and black pepper.
4. **Steam the Mussels:**
    - Add the cleaned mussels to the pot. Cover with a lid and cook for 5-7 minutes, or until the mussels have opened. Shake the pot occasionally to ensure even cooking.
    - Discard any mussels that do not open after cooking.
5. **Finish the Dish:**
    - Stir in the chopped fresh parsley and adjust the seasoning with salt and pepper if needed.
    - Remove the pot from heat.
6. **Serve:**
    - Ladle the mussels and broth into bowls.
    - Garnish with additional fresh parsley if desired.
    - Serve with lemon wedges and crusty bread for dipping into the flavorful broth.

Tips:

- **For Extra Flavor:** Add a splash of cream to the broth for a richer, more decadent sauce.
- **For a Slight Kick:** Add a pinch of red pepper flakes when cooking the garlic and onion.
- **For a More Robust Broth:** Consider adding a splash of seafood stock or a few saffron threads for a deeper flavor.

Enjoy your Oregon White Wine Mussels, a delightful and elegant dish that's perfect for any occasion!

Hazelnut-Crusted Trout

Ingredients:

- **For the Trout:**

- 4 trout fillets (about 6 ounces each), skin on or off as preferred
- 1 cup hazelnuts, finely chopped
- 1/2 cup panko breadcrumbs
- 1/4 cup all-purpose flour
- 2 large eggs
- Salt and black pepper to taste
- 1 tablespoon olive oil (for cooking)

- **For the Breading Station:**
    - 1/2 cup all-purpose flour
    - 2 large eggs, beaten
    - 1 cup finely chopped hazelnuts
    - 1/2 cup panko breadcrumbs
- **For Garnish (optional):**
    - Lemon wedges
    - Fresh parsley or thyme, chopped

Instructions:

1. **Prepare the Breading Station:**
    - Set up three shallow dishes for breading: one with flour, one with beaten eggs, and one with a mixture of finely chopped hazelnuts and panko breadcrumbs.
    - Season the flour with a bit of salt and pepper.
2. **Coat the Trout:**
    - Season the trout fillets with salt and black pepper.
    - Dredge each fillet in the flour, shaking off any excess.
    - Dip the floured fillet into the beaten eggs, ensuring it is fully coated.
    - Press the fillet into the hazelnut-panko mixture, making sure to coat it evenly on all sides.
3. **Cook the Trout:**
    - Heat the olive oil in a large skillet over medium heat.
    - Once the oil is hot, add the trout fillets, skin-side down (if using skin-on).
    - Cook for about 4-5 minutes per side, or until the crust is golden brown and the trout is cooked through. The internal temperature should reach 145°F (63°C).
    - Be careful not to overcrowd the skillet; you may need to cook the fillets in batches.
4. **Serve:**
    - Transfer the cooked trout fillets to a serving platter.
    - Garnish with lemon wedges and fresh herbs if desired.
    - Serve immediately.

Tips:

- **For Extra Crispiness:** Toast the hazelnuts in a dry skillet over medium heat before chopping them to enhance their flavor and crunch.

- **For a More Flavorful Crust:** Add a pinch of dried herbs (such as thyme or rosemary) to the hazelnut-panko mixture.
- **For a Light Sauce:** Serve with a light lemon beurre blanc or a simple garlic lemon butter sauce.

Enjoy your Hazelnut-Crusted Trout, a delicious and elegant dish with a delightful nutty crunch!

Raspberry Lemon Bars

Ingredients:

- **For the Crust:**
    - 1 ½ cups all-purpose flour
    - ½ cup granulated sugar
    - ¼ teaspoon salt
    - ½ cup unsalted butter, cold and cut into small pieces
- **For the Lemon Filling:**
    - 4 large eggs
    - 1 ½ cups granulated sugar
    - 1/3 cup all-purpose flour
    - 1 teaspoon baking powder
    - ½ cup freshly squeezed lemon juice (about 2-3 lemons)
    - 1 tablespoon lemon zest
    - 1 cup fresh raspberries (or frozen, thawed and drained)
- **For the Topping:**
    - Powdered sugar, for dusting (optional)

Instructions:

1. **Prepare the Crust:**
    - Preheat your oven to 350°F (175°C). Grease and line an 8x8-inch baking pan with parchment paper, leaving an overhang for easy removal.
    - In a medium bowl, combine the flour, granulated sugar, and salt.
    - Cut in the cold butter using a pastry cutter or your fingers until the mixture resembles coarse crumbs.
    - Press the mixture evenly into the bottom of the prepared pan to form the crust.
    - Bake the crust in the preheated oven for 15 minutes, or until it is lightly golden.
2. **Prepare the Lemon Filling:**
    - In a large bowl, whisk together the eggs and granulated sugar until smooth and well combined.
    - Add the flour and baking powder, and whisk until the mixture is smooth.
    - Stir in the lemon juice and lemon zest until fully incorporated.
3. **Assemble the Bars:**
    - After the crust has baked for 15 minutes, remove it from the oven and pour the lemon filling over the hot crust.
    - Drop the fresh raspberries evenly over the top of the lemon filling. They may sink slightly into the filling.
4. **Bake the Bars:**
    - Return the pan to the oven and bake for an additional 25-30 minutes, or until the filling is set and the edges are lightly golden. A toothpick inserted into the center should come out clean.
5. **Cool and Serve:**
    - Allow the bars to cool completely in the pan on a wire rack.
    - Once cooled, use the parchment paper to lift the bars out of the pan and cut them into squares.

- Dust with powdered sugar if desired before serving.

Tips:

- **For Extra Flavor:** Add a bit of vanilla extract to the lemon filling for a richer taste.
- **For a Smooth Filling:** Ensure that the lemon juice and zest are well integrated into the filling mixture to avoid any lumps.
- **For Neat Cuts:** Chill the bars in the refrigerator for a few hours before cutting to make them easier to slice.

Enjoy your Raspberry Lemon Bars, a delightful blend of sweet raspberries and tangy lemon that's sure to be a hit with family and friends!